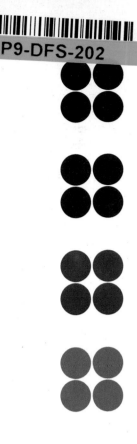

feng shui your life

feng shui your life

jayme barrett

photography by jonn coolidge
foreword by mary steenburgen

Sterling Publishing Co., Inc.
New York

editor: danielle truscott
photographer: jonn coolidge
illustrator: rubén esparza
book designer: lauren monchik
cover: architecture and interior design by tsao mckown (see p. 272)

Library of Congress Cataloging-in-Publication Data
Barrett, Jayme, 1967-
feng shui your life / Jayme Barrett.
     p. cm.
 Includes index.
 ISBN 0-8069-7629-2
 1. Feng shui. I. Title.
BF1779.F4 B365 2003
133.3'337—dc21

                         2002015508

10 9 8 7 6 5 4 3

Published by Sterling Publishing Co., Inc.
387 Park Avenue South, New York, NY 10016
© 2003, Jayme Barrett
Distributed in Canada by Sterling Publishing
C/o Canadian Manda Group, One Atlantic Avenue, Suite 105
Toronto, Ontario, Canada M6K 3E7
Distributed in Great Britain by Chrysalis Books Group PLC,
The Chrysalis Building, Bramley Road, London W10 6SP, England.
Distributed in Australia by Capricorn Link (Australia) Pty. Ltd.
P.O. Box 704, Windsor, NSW 2756, Australia

Manufactured in China
All rights reserved

Sterling ISBN 0-8069-7629-2

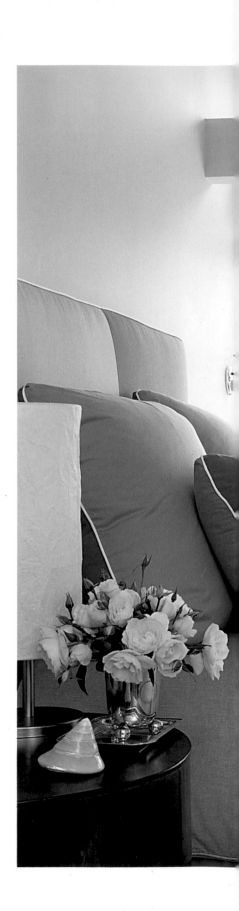

table of contents

foreword

In a way, I have been a student of feng shui ever since I was born. My feng shui "masters" were my mother, Nell Steenburgen, and her sister, Lillian Grimes. The homes that they created were filled with laughter and beauty. Our house was tiny, but you felt good the second that you entered it. My aunt's house, an hour and a half away, was so beautiful to me that I couldn't wait to take friends there to show it off. Neither my mother nor aunt had any kind of formal education in decoration. Likewise, money had nothing to do with what they created. To this day, they probably haven't heard of feng shui. Yet they intuitively practiced many of the suggestions that are beautifully presented in the book that you are about to read. There are lots of definitions of feng shui, but I see it as a sort of harnessing of grace.

The problem with studying a discipline such as feng shui is that it can feel like —well, a discipline. Not with this book, though. My feng shui consultant, Jayme Barrett, has a wealth of knowledge about her subject, but she doesn't expect you to put your house up for auction if some aspect of its design is out of synch with feng shui principles. Her sense of humor and her practicality about what can be changed and what can't is what sets this book apart from others. She goes beyond the traditional aspects of feng shui to share her beautiful sensibilities about how powerfully our thoughts and our words affect what we manifest in life. (One of my favorite passages describes an African tradition in which the phrase "This is a story that doesn't need to happen" is used to rid oneself of nagging negative thoughts. I have shared it with many other parents whose worrying imaginations often drive them crazy!)

Feng Shui Your Life is informative, thorough — and fun, which, really, is what feng shui should be. Most readers will be amazed at how, instinctively, they have always decorated their homes according to feng shui principles. This beautiful book will validate your own sensual instincts and teach you some wonderful new ideas as well. Enjoy!

mary steenburgen

acknowledgements

This book is dedicated to my beautiful mom, Merrily...your loving, vibrant energy blesses each day of my life. I am eternally grateful for your guidance and inspired by your profound wisdom.

Feng Shui Your Life has materialized with the help of many talented, committed and supportive people. My heartfelt appreciation for their energy and inspiration is immeasurable. I am deeply thankful to the following people:

Grand Master Choa Kok Sui, for opening my heart to the power of feng shui and bestowing a lifetime of priceless teachings and blessings; Master Stephen Co, for his spiritual guidance and practical advice; Marie Garcia, for teaching me feng shui essentials; and the late Swami Muktananda, who sparked my passion for meditation and divine energy as a young girl.

My family and friends: my dad, Bob Heck, for his love, kindness, support, and enduring faith in me; my sister, Romi Laine, for her amazing insight, dedication and generosity, and for enhancing my words; Brielle, Alex, and my father Steven Hoffman, whose love and enthusiasm always spurred me on; Horacio Rodriguez, for his encouragement, feedback, and celebration of each accomplishment; Mary Steenburgen and Ted Danson, who graced my life during the writing of this book in countless ways; Tracy Abrams, Tamara Nobles, Anna Gunn, Sherry Hawkins, Julie Lawrence, Vanessa Paloma, Eileen Grobe, Eric Laneuville, Ebby St. Pierre, Alexis Denisof, Jay Stark, Nick Carrell, Lynne Hayashi, Gary Herbel, and Richard Beale for your love, assistance, humor and fortitude.

All of those who so generously allowed their beautiful homes and offices to be photographed including Jane Gekler, Susan and Lou Piatt, Eletra Casadei, Wendy Katz, Teena Leonardi, Valerie Hiss, Fran and Terry Flanagan, Jeff Ester, and Antonia Hutt. And the many interior designers whose stunning work Jonn Coolidge has photographed over the years and appears in this book to illustrate so beautifully an intuitive sense of feng shui (for more information, see p. 272).

Lincoln Boehm and everyone at Sterling Publishing, especially Charles Nurnberg; and my editor, Danielle Truscott, whose daily wisdom and guidance honed and polished the words, ideas, and visual elements of the book, for her invaluable time, commitment, and vision. To photographer Jonn Coolidge, stylist Warner Walcott, illustrator Rubén Esparza, and designer Lauren Monchik for their creativity and talent.

And last, all of the powers that be, visible and invisible, that have guided me in this creative endeavor; and all of my clients and students, who inspire me each day as their lives transform with the wondrous power of feng shui.

introduction

feng shui (pronounced fung schway) is for everyone. It's about how you live, work, and play. Whether you are young or old, lead a simple or extravagant lifestyle, are a homemaker or professional, live in a big house or small apartment—or favor a traditional, contemporary, or eclectic style—the benefits you'll reap from bringing feng shui into your life are huge and many. This ancient art of placement helps you to arrange your home, office, indoor, and outdoor environments so that your life is harmonious and your dreams are realized to their fullest.

The Chinese characters for the words "feng shui" represent "wind" and "water." They are symbols for creating a gentle flow of energy in your environment. In the same way that blood and oxygen must flow freely and purposefully in your body, so must energy and life force circulate throughout your daily environments. The rooms and spaces you inhabit influence your well being and your opportunities in life. Feng shui provides practical methods to strengthen the positive energy in your surroundings and to create beauty. It gives you techniques to transform your home into a sanctuary: a place where you feel happy, healthy, and motivated, where your aspirations become reality. Your daily stress can be greatly reduced when you minimize the chaos of the outside world by creating your own safe haven. When your surroundings nourish you, your energy increases and you feel most empowered to achieve your goals. By infusing your environment with vibrant energy and symbols of beauty, love, success and bounty, your space becomes a living, breathing manifestation of the life you want to live: a blueprint for your destiny.

Feng Shui Your Life provides a holistic approach to feng shui. In addition to décor and interior design ideas based on feng shui elements, this book offers a new way of interacting with the world around you. Feng shui can be a lifestyle. From my point of view, arranging your environment is one piece of the puzzle. It is a beginning; an entry into a new way of discovering how energy affects you on a daily basis. As you interact with and personalize your environment, you connect with your inner aspirations. I believe that in order to change your life, you must breathe new energy into the way you think, speak, act, work, love and, of course, design your surroundings. Shifting your perceptions, attitudes, and behaviors immediately influences your actions. Your actions create your destiny. When you learn to combine the inner and outer feng shui techniques, you'll soon see positive changes in your life.

here's what you'll find in the following chapters:

- The basic principles of feng shui and how they translate into your entire life.
- How to use the Bagua, a feng shui map, to locate the energy centers in your home and office so that you can properly energize each one to enhance your health, relationships, career, finances, family, creativity, wisdom, reputation, and helpful people.
- How to implement feng shui room by room, beginning at the front entrance and moving through the foyer, bedrooms, bathrooms, kitchen, dining room, living room, office and even the garage.
- Loads of feng shui tips and shortcuts that create immediate, transformative changes in your home and life.

I am grateful for the gifts of feng shui and for the guidance of my teacher, Grand Master Choa Kok Sui. After learning and incorporating these techniques, my life transformed exponentially. For me, the gift of feng shui continues and multiplies every day. Because of this, it has become my passion to share it with as many people as possible. So, prosper and enjoy your wondrous journey.

jayme barrett

one: feng shui essentials

Feng shui is about correct energy flow. It applies to your health, work, and relationships, as well as to your everyday interactions. As with any ancient, holistic art, the idea of practicing feng shui—two little words that conjure up a big approach to living—can seem a little intimidating at first. Yet, at its core, feng shui is simply about feeling good and prospering in your life.

Like yoga and meditation, feng shui is rooted in rich traditions and has been studied and applied for thousands of years. Still, you shouldn't feel overwhelmed by the prospect of starting to transform your life with feng shui. In fact, as you sail through this book, you may discover that in some ways you have been instinctively employing feng shui all along.

The aim of this book is to teach you how to feel happier, healthier, and more fulfilled by incorporating feng shui into all facets of your daily life, but don't expect to build Rome – or your new feng shui home – in a day. The good news is that you can begin this process by something as simple as moving a plant from one corner to another, changing the color of your pillows, or buying a few candles to brighten a spot in a room. Whether your motivation is to improve your relationships, finances, career, creativity, wisdom, or reputation or to feel more in touch with yourself and the world around you, you need to know some basic feng shui principles. This chapter will give you the ground rules and start you down the exciting path of using feng shui to achieve your goals easily and joyfully.

The next few pages will introduce you to four categories of feng shui. Although each aspect is distinct, you'll discover that they are all interconnected. Feng shui is based on the idea that everything in your outer surroundings affects the course of your life. Likewise, your inner thoughts, words, and actions make a huge difference in creating your destiny. These complementary ideas work best when you implement them simultaneously. This book will guide you to unite the inner and outer facets of your life to facilitate positive transformation in an integrated way.

The four levels of feng shui you will learn, practice, and blend into your life are:
practical feng shui – The logical and sensible methods of arranging your environment for happiness and success

PREVIOUS PAGE: A living room filled with natural light, fresh flowers, and the soft green color of nature creates positive energy—a great start to a harmonious feng shui lifestyle.

ABOVE: Every color creates its own vibration in your home. Soft pastel pillows calm while vibrant reds and oranges stimulate.

RIGHT: A clean table gives you the opportunity for a peaceful, healthy meal. Fragrant flowers and a lovely view heighten your dining experience.

energy feng shui – The manner in which subtle energy moves through each space you inhabit and affects your life

symbolic feng shui – How the contents of your home and workplace reflect who you are and where you are going

personal feng shui – How your physical, emotional, mental, and spiritual energy influences your path to fulfillment

As you begin to implement feng shui, you will see that each technique encompasses one or more of these attributes. Sometimes a technique utilizes all of them. To achieve optimal results in your life, you'll want to employ feng shui on many levels. For example, imagine your dining room table is a mess. It is strewn with dirty dishes, unpaid bills, and your car keys hidden under junk mail – along with an important document you need for work. As you will soon discover, clutter is one of the biggest deterrents to creating good feng shui in your life. Clearing clutter is a tool that falls into all four categories. From a practical point of view, cleaning off the dining table will save you time because you will be able to find your keys, and it will give you confidence that your document will be safe from food stains and other mess. From an energy standpoint, clutter stops the flow of energy and causes a feeling of chaos. Symbolically, a dining table full of "stuff" says a lot about you. It may indicate that you feel overwhelmed or disorganized or that you don't deserve to nourish yourself in a beautiful environment. It may also suggest that you feel inundated by all the unpaid bills. On a personal level, your energy becomes depleted as you procrastinate cleaning up the clutter. Sometimes you end up using more energy stressing over your unfinished tasks than you would if you took a few minutes to accomplish them. Simply cleaning up, putting everything in its correct spot, and placing fresh flowers in the center of the table can be food for your soul. Keeping your dining area tidy can promote a delightful morning filled with peace and clarity. It also provides you with a nice spot to eat a healthy breakfast that enhances your productivity all day long. This is good feng shui in action.

 ## practical feng shui

Feng shui originated in ancient China, but you can easily implement it in practical and modern ways in your daily life. The ideas presented here are

universal and apply to a wide range of cultures and backgrounds. Because feng shui is not a religion, it does not interfere with any spiritual beliefs. It is used to create positive energy, internally and externally, in a way that nurtures you and your life goals. Throughout the book, you will learn practical ways to influence the shape your life is taking.

Everyone has his or her own unique preferences when it comes to home décor. You really don't need to embrace oriental design elements. Although some feng shui books include only traditional Chinese cures, this book will concentrate on offering solutions that are attractive to a wide range of styles and tastes. For example, in classical texts, Chinese red firecrackers are used to attract attention and to lift your reputation, yet a red candle or a red bulb inside a lamp will create the same energy effect. Be assured that you will receive a myriad of suggestions so you can feel comfortable in your own space. Ultimately, you must love your home and everything inside it. By the way, "home" encompasses every type of dwelling including houses, apartments, condominiums, guesthouses, dorm rooms, and trailers. By the end of the book, the space you live in will be a sanctuary that replenishes your soul and supports your dreams.

Many times, what feels and looks good to you happens to be good feng shui. Because common sense usually dictates how you set up your home, practical feng shui will seem familiar to you. Even if you haven't yet implemented the techniques, you will say to yourself, "That's obvious," or "That makes sense." For example, displaying photos of an ex-spouse or gifts from that person is not good feng shui. If you want to create new love in your life, you should remove anything that reminds you of the past relationship. You want your mind and heart free to love again. Although at times it may be difficult to let go, you must distance yourself from past events, memories, and emotions that are tied up with that person. You do not want to be constantly surrounded by your ex-partner's energy. If you think about it, this makes sense, and yet it is astounding how many people continue to display such items for their sentimental or dollar value.

steps to a happier life

Westerners grasp feng shui when they put the practical validity of the principles to the test. For people who must "see it to believe it," the following examples might influence their ability to embrace feng shui as a viable

tool. In the next week or two, if you want to share your newest feng shui epiphanies at a dinner party, start the discussion with logical, sensible examples as opposed to the more abstract. Feng shui is a stimulating topic of conversation. After reading a few chapters and implementing even the simplest techniques, you might already have experienced changes in your life. You may find yourself emphatically stating that feng shui works while those who have not quite mastered this degree of open-mindedness will be just as convinced that it doesn't. However, even the most scientific of your friends will have to agree with some of the following feng shui principles.

- Clearing clutter is a logical step to accomplish your goals. Keeping your home and workplace clean and organized promotes happiness, efficiency, and peace of mind.
- Finding room for new things in your life requires you to get rid of things you don't use, want, or need. If your bookcase is overloaded with worn, old books from college, you won't have space for fresh, stimulating works that can inspire and educate you to achieve your present and future goals. "Out with the old and in with the new" makes sense.
- Adding sunlight to an environment lifts your spirit and expands your vision; darkness inhibits life force and can be depressing. Bright light is synonymous with birth, creativity, and productivity. Darkness is associated with constriction, hibernation, and sadness.
- Bringing nature indoors adds harmony and healing to the surroundings. Studies have proven that plants produce oxygen and remove carbon dioxide, helping people to feel better. The gentle sound of a water fountain eases your mind, blocks out disturbing noises, and calms your nerves.
- Using different colors can influence your mood. Red and orange tend to stimulate and excite you; blue, green, and lavender calm and relax you.
- Working in the bedroom is not a good idea. The bedroom is a place for rest and connection. You'll want to remove all work-related items such as computers and bills so you can leave the stressful day behind and concentrate on relaxation, quiet contemplation, or intimacy with your partner.

LEFT: Create a sense of calm in the bedroom with neutral-colored linens and plenty of natural light. Purple flowers add a vibrant touch.

- Displaying pictures of you and your loved ones looking happy, healthy, and confident will bring a smile to your face. Everyone in your home will feel the positive energy emanating from the photos.

All of these ideas are consistent with good feng shui. You can benefit from implementing the practical suggestions throughout the book, and you may decide you want to start with them since they make sense. Respect your own pace and always check to see what feels right to you.

energetic feng shui

Feng shui is based on the idea that everything is energy, therefore "energetic." The idea of subtle energy can be a mysterious one since we in the West are so focused on hard, cold evidence. Let's try to make this easier to understand. The world and everything in it is composed of vital energy or life force that vibrates at different frequencies. It swirls in and around every living being in nature, in buildings, and in space. Energy from the sun, earth, and air breathes life force into everyone and everything. Depending on the density of the energy, you may be able to see it. However, even if you can't see it, it exists. For example, you can see water as you pour it into a teapot. However, when you boil it, it turns into steam and eventually becomes invisible. In the same way, you cannot see electricity, but you know it is working when the lights come on. This energy is called various names in different cultures. It is labeled "chi" in China, "ki" in Japan, and "prana" in India. Basically, it is the universal breath of life that connects everything. We will refer to it as "energy."

Energy permeates your physical body and the buildings where you live and work. Your personal energy is constantly interacting with your surroundings and the people and objects within it. You and every object in your daily life have the ability to absorb, project, and deflect energy. In fact, you may be surprised to find out that your dining table, plants, bedspread, and antique watch all contain their own energy field. This is where feng shui enters the picture.

Since you are continually affected by the energy around you, the energy must be healthy and life affirming. If it is physically, emotionally, mentally,

LEFT: Every book, object, and piece of furniture in your home exudes energy that affects you. A study decorated with antiques contains the energy of previous owners; it is important to choose antiques wisely.

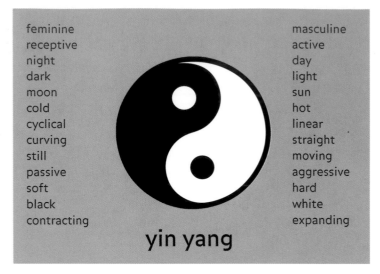

yin and yang

In Chinese philosophy, balance and harmony manifest when the two polar energy forces of yin and yang exist simultaneously within everything in the universe. They dance between each other. One does not exist without the other. In feng shui, your home is meant to combine both yin and yang energies. They complement one another to achieve harmony. For instance, a soft pillow cushions a hard chair, or light place mats brighten a dark table.

feminine	masculine
receptive	active
night	day
dark	light
moon	sun
cold	hot
cyclical	linear
curving	straight
still	moving
passive	aggressive
soft	hard
black	white
contracting	expanding

yin yang

or spiritually toxic, you will experience negative consequences. Imagine a goldfish. The salesman at the pet shop swears that he has the healthiest fish in the city. You take the goldfish home with all the fixings for a great aquarium. What would happen if you put this healthy fish in contaminated water? Is it likely to survive? Well, that depends on the amount of poison that it takes in. Placing your fish in clean water might give it a better chance to survive.

This is what you want to do in your life. Changing the energy in your environment influences the way you feel, think, love, work, and play. Feng shui teaches you how to redirect unhealthy energy and replace it with positive energy that will support your physical, emotional, financial, and spiritual health.

Healthy energy is moving energy. Like water, it needs to flow and circulate to be beneficial. A river moves easily and gently in and around rocks and other natural elements. Flowing water allows fish to remain healthy; stagnant water breeds mosquitoes. Similarly, the blood in your veins, the air in your lungs, the food in your digestive tract, and the synapses in your brain must circulate for optimum health. If they become stagnant, depleted, or congested, your physical condition deteriorates immediately, just as your emotions do. If you hold in your feelings, you may become hurt, angry, or resentful. Sharing feelings with loved ones is cathartic. It immediately opens up the relationship to new levels of intimacy and trust.

By the same token, feng shui offers specific rules to guide the vital energy evenly and continually through your space. As you begin to understand how the tools work, you will become excited with your ability to assess an energy situation and to decide how you will fix it. If you feel blocked in your life, you might simply need to clear the path of any obstructions so that fresh energy can move freely in and around you.

the energy of your home

Your home must have the optimal flow of positive energies to regenerate and propel your life forward. Your home is not simply a place to crash after a long day at work. Like the fish in its water, you are swimming in pools of energy as you interact with your environment. Your dwelling, including the physical structure and every object within it, contains an energy field. The color of the walls, the size of your sofa, the wood floors, the plumbing and electricity, the amount of sunlight, the smells and tastes, the garden and water elements, the photos and artwork affect you on a daily basis.

Each item has an energy field that continually interacts with your personal energy. Imagine an invisible energy cord running from your solar plexus (the soft part between your ribs) to every object you own and to every person you encounter. The cord is like a cable that sends signals to you at every moment. You are either uplifted or depleted by every interaction. Thus, you must be careful about what and whom you bring into your home. If you have to swim in the energy, it needs to be positive, or you may be sabotaging yourself.

In addition, your home contains emotional energies created by the previous tenants and by you. Every thought, emotion, and

BELOW: Brightly colored beanbags and playful artwork convey a youthful energy, while a telescope represents a promising future.

21

activity that has been experienced in the house is part of your home's energy field. If you and those who lived in your home have met with happiness and success, you are in luck. However, if the former owners had physical, mental, or financial hardship, you must cleanse the area of all negative energies. In many cases, you have no way of finding out what fortune or misfortune the previous owners or tenants had, so it's a good idea to clean all spaces before you inhabit them. Recognizing that the energy in your home has everything to do with the energy in your life is fundamental. Dwellings that radiate love, happiness, and fortuity present those same feelings and opportunities for you.

symbolic feng shui

Along with correct energy flow, you need to be keenly aware of what your house is saying to you on a daily basis. Symbolic feng shui is based on the idea that the contents of your home reflect who you are. Your house serves as a mirror for your thoughts, passions, morals, spiritual beliefs, hobbies, and much more. One of the exciting aspects of feng shui is that you can change what your home is saying to you. As you change the outer template of your home to encourage your unique dreams and goals, your inner life shifts. Becoming clear about your dreams and goals for health, love, happiness, and success and using symbols for them within your environment is essential. When your intention for your life surrounds you, it tends to materialize in a better and faster way.

If you look around your house objectively, what kind of person would you say lives there? You might want to ask yourself some questions. Judging from the pictures on the wall, style of furniture, condition of the yard, colors, tidiness, and your personal mementos, what can you determine about yourself? Is your environment in alignment with how you see yourself and what you want? Does your home exude success, confidence, health, and love? Consider which rooms you feel most comfortable in and which you avoid. If toys have taken over the living room, this may leave you with no space to complete your own creative projects. If the kitchen is devoid of food, perhaps you aren't taking time to nourish yourself. If your bedroom is the most beautiful room in the home, rest and relaxation may be high on your list of values.

RIGHT: Our homes are filled with symbols that continually affect us. Artwork with encouraging words such as "New Vistas" offers a daily positive affirmation.

In addition, the different components making up your home represent certain aspects of your life. The electricity, plumbing, roof, walls, and floors correspond to your inner workings. The following are some examples of how your home might reflect what is happening in your life. Explore other possibilities by coming up with your own meanings as well.

- Electricity stands for your life force, your own inner spark. If you find yourself in the dark without electricity, you may feel depleted or unable to function. Circuit breakers that regularly blow might hint that you feel overloaded and need to relax more.
- The plumbing represents your feelings because water is associated with your emotional life. If the drains are clogged, you might find that you are holding in your feelings. A toilet that constantly overflows may indicate that your emotions are overwhelming and spilling out right and left.
- The roof and walls symbolize security and support. Don't let your roof become dilapidated, or you may feel insecure that your life is caving in on you. If your walls have holes, cracks, or peeling paint, you may feel as if your support systems are coming apart at the seams.
- The floors represent your grounding and stability. Floorboards should be strong, or you might feel unsure about the ground you are walking on in your life.

objects and their meaning

Every object in your life has a memory association as well as an energy attachment that consciously or unconsciously affects you. These are represented by two types of symbolism. The face-value symbolism is the obvious one. A piece of art that portrays starving children in a third-world country elicits a specific kind of reaction. A photo of a colorful garden in France inspires a very different set of thoughts and responses. At face value, you can make quick determinations as to what kind of energy each item in your home is radiating.

The other type of symbolism is connected with your personal thoughts, feelings, and memories. Every object comes with a history – a history of where you bought it, who you were with, who might have given it to you, what your relationship is or was with that person, if you like the object, if it was expensive, and what was happening in your life at the time. That is a lot of information for you to process instantaneously. Most of the time, you are not

RIGHT: A simple seashell collection can possess many meanings. Shells may remind you of time spent with a loved one, happy summer days, or the life-giving energy of the ocean.

even aware of how each object affects you. Decorate your space with happy and joyous objects. Certainly, a surplus of upsetting ones will bring you down. You must understand that energy, positive or negative, reverberates through every cell of your body and constantly influences your emotions.

As we discussed earlier, you are attached to each object by an invisible energy cord. Each memento, photo, bath product, book, chair, and CD is saying something about you and to you. As you look around your home, review one object at a time. Ask yourself if it makes you happy or sad. What is your first thought or reaction? Does this item bring you joy or do you despise it? Did a loved one give it to you? What is your current relationship with that person? Is it keeping you stuck in the past or moving you forward? Who owned it previously? Inherited items, antiques, and objects from previous marriages have the energy of the people who owned them. Since you know that each item carries the energy imprint of the owner, pay special attention to those particular items in your home. In chapter three, you will learn how to purify the energy surrounding objects. You should give yourself permission to put away items that deplete you or that make you feel melancholy. Feng shui encourages you to keep only those objects that bring you joy, love, and happiness.

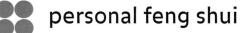 ## personal feng shui

Your life is complete when you integrate balance, flow, and positive energy into your body, mind, and spirit using the principles of feng shui. Your health is precious; without it, you cannot wholeheartedly enjoy a harmonious existence or the material pleasures of life. As you incorporate feng shui into your home, promise yourself that you will replenish your personal energy at the same time. Taking care of your physical, emotional, mental, and spiritual life is predicated on how much fresh energy you can bring in and circulate through your body. Whether you are eating healthy foods, expressing your feelings, stimulating your mind, or finding peace through spiritual practice, energy is in motion. Sometimes too much energy exists in a specific area, causing congestion; at other times, you are not getting enough energy. You feel depleted, and it's important to bring in more.

From a personal standpoint, you need to do the "inner work" while you make the physical changes to your home. Plants in your front entrance help stimulate the energy of health, but you won't get in shape by simply walking past them on the way to the couch. Creating the right internal conditions in your mental, emotional, and spiritual life will open the door to ease and contentment. Happiness and fulfillment come from within. Fortunately, there are wonderful techniques and tools to bring them closer to your heart, and, in the next chapter, you will have the opportunity to do so.

your energy field

An invisible electromagnetic energy field surrounds you and is connected to your physical body. This energy field is sometimes referred to as an "aura." Every living thing has an aura. At times in your life, you may have sensed someone's aura – in other words, you felt an instant rapport or chemistry with the person after only a few words. Within your aura are energy centers called "chakras." (In ancient Sanskrit, chakra means "wheel of light.") The chakras are constantly spinning and absorbing currents of energy. In her book *Why People Don't Heal and How They Can*, Caroline Myss refers to chakras as "computer disks imprinted with information." Chakras control specific organs and systems in the physical body as well as psychological functions in the emotional body. When you keep yourself physically and emotionally balanced with healthy foods, exercise, yoga, and meditation, your chakras stay in good working condition. When you maintain a vibrant energy field, your health will thrive.

Traditional Eastern philosophy refers to seven major chakras located from the base of the spine to the top of the head. However, in his book, *Miracles Through Pranic Healing*, Master Choa Kok Sui suggests that there are eleven major chakras. These act like "power stations" to the vital organs. Pranic healing, an ancient healing modality that has been modernized by Choa Kok Sui, uses "prana" or "life force energy" to heal the physical body as well as psychological illnesses.

RIGHT: The human energy field, or aura, is comprised of eleven major chakras that correspond to physical and psychological functions in the body.

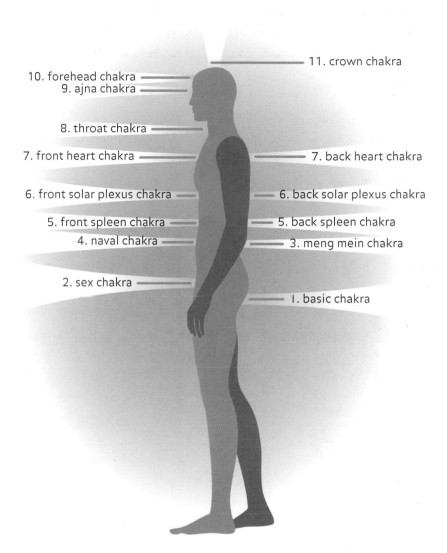

11. crown chakra
10. forehead chakra
9. ajna chakra
8. throat chakra
7. front heart chakra
7. back heart chakra
6. front solar plexus chakra
6. back solar plexus chakra
5. front spleen chakra
5. back spleen chakra
4. naval chakra
3. meng mein chakra
2. sex chakra
1. basic chakra

As stated above, each chakra has physical and emotional functions. For instance, on a physical level, the basic chakra located at the base of the spine corresponds to the muscular and skeletal systems and to general vitality. The front solar plexus affects the internal organs such as the pancreas, liver, diaphragm, large intestines, stomach, lungs, and heart. Psychologically, while the heart chakra deals with your physical heart and thymus gland, it also influences and is affected by your higher emotions. In the same way, the throat chakra corresponds to your throat, thyroid gland, and lymphatic system while simultaneously affecting your ability to communicate your needs, desires, and creativity in a detailed manner. Implementing good feng shui in your surroundings will increase your personal energy because your surroundings are constantly interacting with your chakras. A healthy energy field leads to vitality in your body, mind, and spirit and ultimately supports you in living a productive life.

stress relief

Cleaning the energy field is the key to your overall health. If not taken care of, everyday stress can pave the way for more serious ailments. Disease occurs as an irregularity in the energy body. You have a higher probability of becoming physically or emotionally run-down when the chakras become

a healing salt bath

Remember how you felt the last time you took a swim in the ocean? You probably felt both refreshed and exhilarated. Simulate the experience and cleanse yourself at the same time by taking a few baths every week.

- Draw a warm bath and put one to two pounds of sea salt (two to four cups) in the water.
- Add ten drops of lavender essential oil or another type that pleases you.
- Relax in the salt bath for at least twenty minutes.
- Make sure that the majority of your body is covered with the salt water at some point during bathing.
- Visualize healing white light filling your entire body. Imagine that the light is flushing all physical, emotional, and mental stress out of your hands and feet and being disintegrated immediately.
- Say, "Thank you for cleansing and healing my whole body now!" three times.
- If you do not have a bathtub, rub the salt over your body after you've been in the shower for a bit and your body is moist. Rinse after five to ten minutes.

LEFT: A big, old-fashioned tub is perfect for a salt-water bubble bath. After soaking for twenty minutes and doing a healing visualization at day's end, you will head to bed feeling lighter and happier.

dirty, congested, or depleted. When you create a strong energy blueprint for the body, your physical health will follow it. You must clean before you energize. You wouldn't mix fresh milk with spoiled milk in an attempt to clean up the impurities. The logical approach would be to dump the milk, wash the glass, and then pour a fresh glass. The principle is the same when dealing with your energy field. Clean it first; then, it will be open and available to receive new vitality from the sun, earth, and air.

An effective way to clean your own energy field is by jumping in the ocean or by taking a saltwater bath. For centuries, salt has been used for cleansing and purification. It has the ability to disintegrate negativity, cleanse your energy field, and increase the energy circulation in all of your chakras. Every day, thousands of people still flock to the Dead Sea for its natural healing properties. The water absorbs dirty energy, and the salt immediately breaks down negative physical, emotional, and mental residue. If you want the same effect in your home, use sea salt or regular table salt in your bath water. Adding essential oils will further the healing process and make the water silky. The best essential oils for cleaning dirty energy are lavender, tea tree, and eucalyptus.

your personal color palette

Color is splashed around you and affects your daily life in many ways. Heightening your awareness about color helps you to use it effectively to enhance your health and well-being. Wherever you go, you are surrounded by colors that heal, invigorate, harmonize, or relax. Colors associated with a particular holiday such as Christmas immediately remind you of wonderful times shared with loved ones. Other colors evoke visions of natural elements such as the sun, ocean, grass, or roses. Each color stimulates a different response within you. Once you determine how each color affects your energy, moods, and emotions, you will be able to make powerful choices to influence your life in a more positive way.

You have control of the colors in your clothes, food, and your home. Keep in mind that having a little of every color is a balanced way of bringing vibrant energy into your life. Experiment by integrating new ones into your wardrobe and food choices. If you notice that black is the mainstay in your clothing and décor, mix in colorful accessories to brighten them up. For example, yellow uplifts, pink softens, and green adds a healing touch. In fact, eating a colorful

red	pink	orange	green	yellow	gold	blue	violet	brown	black	white
passion	love	enthusiasm	harmony	optimism	wealth	imagination	intuition	solidity	strength	purity
courage	sweetness	joy	beginnings	focus	wisdom	calm	devotion	warmth	elegance	innocence
power	uplift	exuberance	prosperity	communication	luxury	serenity	respect	practicality	protection	faith
wealth	happiness	interaction	nature	sunshine	abundance	relaxation	peace	diligence	sophistication	benevolence
motivation	tenderness	fun	growth	inspiration	sparkle	compassion	spirituality	reliability	intelligence	honesty
fame	enticement	captivation	healing	fidelity	influence	ocean	awareness	patience	shrewdness	grace

LEFT: Integrate pleasing colors into your wardrobe and environment to uplift your spirit, enliven your home, or accentuate a desired feeling or yearning.

salad with lettuce, red cabbage, carrots, tomatoes, cucumbers, corn, and garbanzo beans can give you physical and soulful nourishment in the same bite. Throughout the book, you will learn how color plays an essential part in bringing the principles of feng shui into your life.

 ## feng shui awareness

Choosing good feng shui in any situation is nothing more than an awareness of what feels right and what doesn't. It's really that easy. Each circumstance, thought, or person will either energize you or deplete you. It's up to you to decide whether it will expand or contract your energy field. Be aware that everything, including your boss, a friend, a dinner party, a conversation, a meal, and your clothing, affects you. Move towards the people and things that make you happy and pass on the ones that don't.

Sometimes, you can base your choices on past events, but many times you'll need to take a risk. For example, if you have a friend who complains endlessly and invariably brings you down, it is safe to say that spending time with that person is not great feng shui. Similarly, staying in a job that squelches your creativity and underpays you is not beneficial. Conversely, if you feel lonely, signing up for a class at a community college is excellent feng shui, even though you are nervous about meeting new people. As you move through each day, make positive choices: go to a happy, feel-good movie; ask your mentor to dinner; play uplifting music; or take a walk on the beach at sunset.

Observe how you feel when spending time with specific people in your life. Include all of your loved ones, colleagues, friends, and neighbors. How do you feel when you're with them, and how do you feel after you leave them? Be aware of your emotional, mental, and physical state when you're in friends' homes, in restaurants, at work, in department stores, at the movies, and at concerts. Are you uplifted or depressed? You have free will to make conscious choices at every moment. Have fun with your new feng shui outlook. Ask yourself, "Is this good feng shui or not?" As you actively and purposefully apply these principles in your everyday life, feng shui will transform the way you think, feel, and act. Ultimately, creating good feng shui, wherever you are, allows you to design your destiny.

Proceed on your journey with excitement and positive expectations. At the same time, be patient. Remain open for transformation to take place in ways you could not have imagined. You may be hoping for a raise, but instead you receive an abundant tax refund. Your path is unique. The timetable for materialization is different for each person. Regardless, your life will flourish as you welcome all feng shui possibilities.

The great yogi Patanjali says, "When you are inspired by some great purpose, some extraordinary project, all of your thoughts break their bonds; your mind transcends limitations; your consciousness expands in every direction; and you find yourself in a great, new, and wonderful world. Dormant forces, faculties, and talents become alive, and you discover yourself to be a greater person by far than you ever dreamed yourself to be."

take action now

At the end of most chapters (and at the ends of each major section in chapters seven, eight, nine, and ten), you will find practical steps you can take to put feng shui into practice. Action is the key to your success. Take small steps towards transforming your home and your life. As you make each shift, you will start to see and feel differences on a daily basis. These differences will inspire you to keep going. Be patient. Try not to get overwhelmed. You can't apply the principles of feng shui to your entire home in one weekend, but you can create change by taking action. Have fun with the process. Set out to build your feng shui potential right now.

1. make at least three to five practical changes that will help you feel happy. You can simply make your bed, do the dishes, take out the trash, place unread newspapers in a recycle bin, remove a broken object from sight, put away photos of people who upset you, and replace them with ones that make you feel loved and confident.

2. pull back the curtains and open the windows to let in sunlight and nature's energy.

3. look around your space and notice the face-value symbolism. What is each specific item radiating? Does each item promote positive or negative thoughts? How does the object make you feel? Make notes of your first impressions.

4. take a salt bath to release stress and to enhance your physical, mental, and emotional well-being.

5. pick out a new color to wear and see how it influences you and others.

6. create a fun plan with your favorite person and enjoy the love, support, and friendship you feel. This experience can remind you of the characteristics of good feng shui.

two: inner feng shui

While feng shui helps you to attain your outward goals and material prosperity, a primary objective is to achieve balance and harmony within yourself and with your surroundings. You need to apply feng shui to your inner life as well as to your outer life. Lasting change occurs when you combine the two. Your consciousness must shift as your home shifts. Become motivated to fill yourself with love, spirit, self-worth, and inner zest while obtaining the material objects you desire most. This will be the best of both worlds.

Do you ever wonder when and where you will tap into true happiness? Many times, you search the world looking for "things" that will magically bring you joy. The pursuit might be fruitless until you realize that contentment comes from inside. The perfect job, spouse, home, and all the money in the world don't necessarily equal inner fulfillment. Don't get me wrong, it can make things a lot easier. Money grants you freedom, but an abundance of "things" can create more stress. You need to be prepared for success in order to achieve and preserve it. Each achievement must be built on a strong foundation. A good head on your shoulders, an open and giving heart, a positive outlook, a spiritual approach, and a solid family unit will support your triumphs.

PREVIOUS PAGE: A hammock provides a wonderful place to capture the present moment and envision your future.

the big questions

Why did you pick up this book? What are you meant to be doing in life? Do you have a weekly, monthly, or yearly plan? How committed are you to transforming your life, starting today? What can you do to make your life extraordinary right now? These are a few questions you might want to ask yourself. Feng shui can help you to materialize health, wealth, love, creativity, and success. Which one of these is most important to you and why? Where is your focus today? What do you want to be focusing on tomorrow? Once you become clear about where you are now and where you want to be, you'll have an easier time connecting the dots.

You may find that your life is a routine that doesn't vary much from day to day. You get up, gobble down breakfast, go to work, come home, eat dinner, and promptly fall into bed. Here and there you work out, take a short vacation, visit with friends and family, but your life is without a short-term or long-term plan. All of a sudden, five years have passed, and you realize that you are yearning for something more. Being inundated by the whirlwind of your career or children can cause you to forget your true calling. Before starting to apply feng shui to your home, get in touch with all of those wonderful dreams you have when no one is looking.

In the following pages, you will find simple recommendations to strengthen your internal feng shui, which is essential to the manifestation process. After you align your thoughts, behaviors, and actions with the

RIGHT: This meandering walkway symbolizes your path to fulfillment. Its wooden planks and abundant plant life remind you to stay grounded as you walk forward in life.

deep desires of your heart and soul, altering your environment with feng shui will be a piece of cake. Your clarity, intention, and determination will lead the way.

your purpose

You are in this world to express your creativity, individuality, and love. What is it that you want to give? How can you fulfill your dreams and help others simultaneously? If you could be anyone or do anything, what would that look like? What is your purpose here on earth? In *Your Infinite Power to Be Rich*, Joseph Murphy states, "You are here to find your true place in life, and to give of your talents to the world. You are here to expand and unfold in a wonderful way, according to your God-given potential, and to bring forth spiritual, mental, and material riches that will bless humanity in countless ways. Learn how to surround yourself always with beauty and luxury, and realize your inalienable right to life, liberty, freedom, and peace of mind. You are not here to earn a mere living. Life is a gift to you."

How can you freely give love, resources, and inspiration when you may be settling for a life that is not gratifying? Now is the time to expand your vision to discover your purpose. Start by honoring your dreams and goals for yourself. If you don't remember them anymore, think back to when you were a child – what did you dream about? When did you feel your best? What were your hobbies? What were you passionate about? You may discover that your dream is closer than you think. Your dream may be motivated by your heart, by pure ambition, or by both. Perhaps you realize that it's staying home with the kids or arranging flowers in your own gift shop. Or it could be your life-long desire to move to another country or to operate your own airline. Your passion is the driving force for creating inner and outer feng shui.

your dreams

When you follow your dreams, you create a new world for yourself and bring others along for the ride. Don't be afraid to verbalize your dreams, fearing that someone might take them away or laugh at them. You should only share them with supportive people. Be willing to take a risk and step out of your comfort zone. Every time you tell yourself that your dream is impossible, you are telling yourself a lie. You open up an infinite space for fear to rush in and take over. Sometimes, the fear is not that you can't do

it, but rather, if you realize your dream, what then? You ask yourself, "What will my life be like if I step out of familiarity and into uncertainty?"

If you don't try something new, you won't get the results you desire. One of the definitions of insanity is doing the same thing over and over again expecting a different result. You are reading this book because you want a change. Be willing to venture into the unknown where the possibilities for your creative endeavors are endless. You must firmly believe your dreams are possible in order for them to manifest. It is never too late to act on them. Start now. You will be one day closer to achieving them.

Dream big and dream in color. Let your imagination run wild. For inner feng shui to take hold, visualize your outcome every day. Watch it play out like a movie. Perhaps you have always wanted to escape city life to raise horses in the country. In your movie, see the sprawling ranch house, smell the grass, taste the fresh lemonade, hear the wind in the trees, and feel the horse gallop beneath you. Envision yourself participating in the activities that make you happy. See yourself smiling and laughing, surrounded by your loved ones. Play this movie over and over again. In chapters five and six, you will learn how to represent this dream in your home so you will see it physically everyday. Blending your mind power with your house power is the key to successful feng shui.

Expand your horizons. Move beyond the normal and mediocre to the extraordinary. Be daring. Ride the waves of life with enthusiasm, passion, and freedom in your heart. Open your arms wide and receive the opportunities that life is presenting you. Be lighthearted. You have much to offer the world. You deserve the very best. Your destiny awaits you; skip towards it.

guidance

Guidance comes to you all day long in many small ways. It comes when you decide to buy one brand of toothpaste over another or when you call your mom exactly when she needs you most. How about when you dream about an elementary school friend and bump into him two hours later at a coffeehouse you have never been to before? He turns out to be a lawyer, and you desperately need one. Is this guidance or synchronicity? It is both. Synchronicity is the exciting moment when people and events come together in an unexpected, but much needed way to uplift your life. Many people wait for guidance to sweep down from above and spell out on a big chalkboard what they are supposed to be doing. It doesn't usually happen that way, and if it did, would you follow it? You obtain guidance when you are ready to receive it.

Guidance comes faster and is clearer when you ask for it. Ask for what you want – be it advice, wisdom, clarity, strength, or love. You might even ask for the best store to purchase a feng shui water fountain and then look in the yellow pages. Make it a practice to ask for help before you go to bed, when you wake up, and definitely prior to an important undertaking.

RIGHT: A favorite chair with cozy pillows near an open window is an ideal spot to listen for inner guidance.

Before an interview, during a speech, and in the middle of a heated discussion, request assistance. Asking is an accelerated way to invite wisdom and grace to flow through you.

The key is to be open and receptive. You must get out of the way so energy can come down and point you in the right direction. The most significant tip is always to say, "Thank you," as if you have already received it. Be sure to ask with reverence and a grateful heart.

two methods of receiving guidance

One way to receive guidance is to be quiet, clear the clutter from your mind, go inside, and listen. Sharpen your listening skills and trust your instincts. That sounds easier than it actually is. There are ways to subdue the thoughts so you can hear what your soul, the universe, nature, or your inner self (whatever name feels right to you) is trying to communicate to you. Salt baths, breathing exercises, and meditation help you to slow down and become aware of the whisperings of your soul. The more you follow your inner guidance, the more it comes to you. With every right action, you feel stronger, freer, and more confident. Have faith that the universe is showing you the way and that you are not alone.

The second way is to be hyperaware of your moment-to-moment thoughts as you go about your day. If you think about paying the rent two to three times in thirty minutes, guidance is probably prompting you to do it. If the image of your dirty car keeps popping into your head, you should get your car washed. You never know who will show up or what information you might overhear. Maybe a magazine article will catch your fancy and give you an idea for a work project. Follow this simple rule: If a particular thought keeps appearing in your head, assume it is guidance and pursue it. In many instances, when you go after it, synchronicity occurs.

the power of breathing

Paying attention to your breathing is one of the fastest ways to become calm, centered, and energized. Have you noticed that when you feel anxious, excited, or fearful, your breathing becomes choppy, quick, and shallow? The key is to breathe fully, deeply, and slowly. As you inhale, let your stomach expand and fill your lungs with air. Do the same as you exhale. Your stomach goes in first, and then your lungs contract as you let the air out. Practicing yoga is a powerful way to become conscious of your breathing and to balance your body, mind, and spirit. If you feel stressed during the day, stop everything and breathe deeply. You will compose yourself, bring in vital energy, and get off the "fast track," if only for a few priceless moments. Breathe properly; then ask for guidance. Your mind will be less jumbled, and you will be able to actually hear the guidance.

breathing exercise from *miracles through pranic healing* by Choa Kok Sui

Pranic breathing is a potent way to bring life force energy into your body. You can use it during meditation, on a walk, or in your car. You can use it to absorb energy in nature. Whenever you are feeling low on energy, practice pranic breathing for twelve cycles, and you will feel refreshed.

- Gently place your tongue on the roof of your mouth. This helps circulate energy throughout the body.
- Inhale through your nose for six counts.
- Hold your breath for three counts.
- Exhale through your nose for six counts.
- Hold your breath for three counts.
- This 6-3-6-3 breathing completes one cycle.

tree energy

Trees radiate an abundance of healing energy into the environment. You can feel a sense of harmony, vitality, and peace when walking among huge trees in the forest and the mountains. You feel alive. People who consistently hug trees have been healed of many illnesses. If you are receptive, it is possible to receive an enormous amount of life energy from a friendly tree in your backyard or in a nearby park. It is fantastic thing to do during a lunch break at work. You may look silly, but it's worth it. Don't underestimate how amazing you will feel after asking a tree to send you some of its extraordinary life force. Here's how:

- Find a large, healthy tree, take off your shoes, and stand or sit underneath it.
- Ask respectfully (silently if you'd like) for some of the tree's excess energy.
- Recite, "Thank you for the healing energy I am receiving right now, I am so grateful."
- Open and close both hands ten times to activate your hand chakras.
- Bend your elbows and raise your hands with your palms facing the tree. Your hands should be about a foot away from the tree. If you like, you can also touch the trunk .
- Do twelve cycles of pranic breathing, following the directions on page 42.
- Imagine the tree's energy filling your hands and circulating through your whole body every time you breathe in. If you are not feeling well in a certain area, imagine that area filled with healing white light.
- Imagine dirty energy, stress, or pain leaving your body through your feet as you exhale.
- Rest under the tree, allowing your body to absorb the energy.
- Give thanks when you are finished. Notice how your energy lifts in the next half-hour.

meditation for inner peace

You can embrace meditation no matter which religious faith or tradition you follow. Silent repetition of a prayer or mantra can help you tame your thoughts and create a calm mind. A mantra is a cosmic word or sound vibration that allows you to deepen your spiritual connection. As you sit for meditation and gently become aware of your breathing, you may want to recite the Sanskrit mantra, Om Namah Shivaya, which means, "I respect the divine energy or God within me." I learned this great mantra from Swami Muktananda who brought Siddha Yoga to the West in the 1970s. I have found that reciting this mantra is beneficial in many circumstances in addition to its use in meditation. Sitting in traffic is one of them.

being still

Meditation is the art of being still, connecting to your spiritual self, and giving full attention to your inner life. With meditation, you can experience joy, serenity, and oneness. As you tame your wild mind, you will find answers to many of your questions by listening to your inner wisdom with an open heart. Imagine that meditation is just another way of turning on the faucet of life-force energy. Every time you sit to meditate you are reactivating the flow. Your intention to be still is important. Some people may not want to sit for a formal meditation; others may not have the time. In either case, just ask reverently for the faucet to be switched on and for guidance to come through. Sit with an attitude of expectancy. Perhaps you will remember someone's words from a week or a year ago that can be applied to an issue you are dealing with today. Give the energy a chance to talk to you.

If you are interested in learning another powerful meditation/visualization, the following one is offered with love. It is a four-part simple meditation you can practice for peace, healing, vitality, clarity, and guidance. It will help you connect with the divine energy within you. You can practice each part separately if you are pressed for time, but it is most effective when you integrate all four steps.

Setting a ritual for meditation prepares you to go inward. You may want to designate a special pillow to sit on, burn candles or incense, and read a passage from an inspirational book to create the right ambiance for meditation. Meditate at the same time every day and preferably in the morning when you are fresh. Do a few stretches, exercises, or yoga or go for a walk beforehand if you'd like. Physical exercise opens up your energy field to receive. With your back straight, find a comfortable position on a chair or sit cross-legged on your pillow on the floor. You must start the meditation by asking for guidance; you end the meditation by expressing gratitude. The following is inspired by various meditations from *Miracles Through Pranic Healing* by Choa Kok Sui.

step 1 – a calm mind

- Invoke for blessings, guidance, peace, protection, and illumination.
- Close your eyes and imagine you are in a beautiful natural setting with trees, mountains, flowers, and blue skies. If you like water, you can imagine yourself floating in a warm lavender lake.
- Practice pranic breathing for ten cycles. As you breathe in, visualize healing energy entering your body. When you breathe out, visualize stress or dirty energy leaving your body through your feet.

step 2 – healing light

- Imagine that your body is an empty bottle. Visualize brilliant white light entering through the top of your head and flushing every cell, every organ, muscle, and bone of your body with healing energy.
- Silently affirm, "The white light is flowing into my head, my brain, my eyes." Continue downward, imagining that each part is purified and energized. Affirm that each part of your body is "healthy and full of light." Repeat this as you visualize every part of your body down to your feet. Imagine the impurities flowing easily out of your feet into the earth.
- Repeat the above exercise with lavender light for increased emotional and mental well-being.

step 3 – the sound of OM

- With your eyes closed, repeat OM silently. This is the universal sound of creation that elevates your consciousness. If thoughts arise, gently bring your attention back to OM.
- Be aware of the moment of silence between each repetition of OM. As you meditate on each gap or pause, you will find inner peace.
- Practice the OM meditation for five to fifteen minutes. Let go, be still, and allow guidance to come through.

step 4 – love and blessings

- Tap your heart a few times (the center of your chest), and imagine a pink rose dwelling inside.
- Visualize people you love in the pink rose; send them love, light, healing, confidence, forgiveness, faith, strength, and prosperity.
- Send love and blessings to the whole earth, especially people and countries in need.
- Send energy to your career and projects. Visualize them blossoming.

• Give thanks for all blessings of love, health, guidance, protection, happiness, and abundance in your life. Open your eyes with a big smile. Do physical exercise to circulate the energy.

your intuition

With all this energy flowing, you will have a much easier time following your intuition. Listen to your heart; it feels good when you are cruising in the right direction. If you make a wrong turn, ask your heart what to do next. Your intuition will guide you in making strong choices. As you read each chapter and begin to actually implement feng shui in your space, intuition will come in handy. Listen to what your home is telling you. Look around and become aware of what needs your attention. If you find yourself avoiding a certain area, piece of furniture, or room, it probably means that you need to pay attention to what is going on there. The old saying, "What you resist, persists," comes to mind.

If you consistently avoid your bookcase, it could indicate that you dislike your books, feel guilty that you don't read enough, or simply can't get yourself to finish them. Perhaps you notice that the majority of your collection is negative. Give yourself a kick in the rear and deal with it. Remove the books that don't work for you. Open the shelf up for new, exciting, passionate material. You will use your intuition over and over as you apply feng shui to each room. Usually, there will be several energy solutions and enhancements for a particular area. Choose the one that suits you and your personal taste. It's better for you to love your space than to have absolutely perfect feng shui everywhere. Use your intuition to listen to your home, sit with the change, and see how it makes you feel.

a pattern of abundance

Creating flow is the essence of feng shui. The universal law, "The more you give, the more you receive," is essential to get energy moving. It implies circulation. For example, try taking a deep breath in, another, and another without exhaling. It is impossible. You must exhale before inhaling again. If you are not giving, then the flow stops and blockages arise. A pattern of abundance is created when you always have more to offer. There is no feeling of lack, only of plenty. In feng shui, the idea is to give energy to your environment in order to receive good fortune back in specific areas of your life, whether it is love, health, wealth, or something else.

It is important to use this principle throughout the book as you manifest your own desires. For all of the goals you achieve, money you bring in, and love you attract, ask yourself, "What can I give back?" "How can I serve?" "How can I help someone else manifest their dream?" If you get a new job, think of ways that you can help others to secure a job. As they say, "What goes around, comes around." That's where the law of karma kicks in. As with physics, for every action, there is a reaction. It is beneficial for you to generate as much good as possible because it will come back to you multiplied many times. You must copiously give that which you desire most. If you want to have a baby, offer to baby-sit a neighbor's child, volunteer at a daycare center, throw a baby shower for a friend. If you want love, you must bestow love abundantly. If you desire more prosperity, share your wealth. The more you want something, the more you must give it. It always comes back to you.

good karma and good feng shui

Karma suggests that your current life is a result of the choices and actions you took in the past. You can neutralize negative karma by giving in the present. In this way, you will be creating a successful future and helping the feng shui to manifest faster. You'll find many ways of giving to help circulate positive energy in your life. Compliments, affection, support, time, and love are all evidence of emotional generosity. This type of giving opens your heart and the hearts of others. Helping people makes you feel kind and creates a feeling inside that you deserve the same. Forgiveness is one of the best ways to create good karma, release the past, and heal upsetting situations. As you forgive others, you will be forgiven. Too much precious energy is wasted holding on to resentments from the past when you could be focusing on moving forward with your life. You are not forgetting what happened or condoning it. By letting go, you are giving yourself emotional freedom.

External giving deals with donating money and gifts. Sometimes, this is difficult for us to do. People wonder how they can give money away when

pink light

Sending pink light from your heart is a wonderful gift to bestow upon everyone, including friends, family, coworkers, people on the news, countries in trouble, and even your enemies. Create good karma; as you send love, you will receive love. This is an effective technique to use before a creative meeting, intimidating phone call, or a blind date. For instance, send pink light for weeks before a job interview. Visualize the scene: getting the job, shaking hands with your new boss, being offered more money than you asked for, and smiling. Finally, blast the whole scene with pink light. Pink energy makes people receptive to you. Utilize it when you have upset someone and desire forgiveness. Use it when a loved one needs encouragement. Think of it as sending a bouquet of energy roses. The pink softens the aura and creates a rapport between your energy and theirs. Both of you will feel great. In addition, they'll respond to you in a positive way and won't know why. It's your secret!

Here's how:
- Close your eyes. Rub the center of your chest and imagine a pink rose within your heart.
- Put your hands up, with bent elbows, facing forward (as if in a lower push-up position).
- Visualize pink energy or light coming from your heart area through your hands to the person or situation. Imagine that a pink cloud envelopes them, and they send it back to you. Think of sending pink cotton candy back and forth.
- Envision the situation exactly as you want it to occur with everyone smiling; keep wrapping the whole scene with pink light from your heart.
- Say to yourself, "I'm sending pink light to this person or situation. May they be blessed with love and sweetness. I'm so grateful that this situation (meeting, phone call, etc) has worked out in the best way possible." You can continue to say your own words. The more specific you are the better.

they are struggling to pay the rent. It's important to do it in whatever small way you can. Give money to get money. Create prosperity consciousness with the awareness that there is always enough. You can summon currents of financial, emotional, and physical delight by giving in the correct way. This is an example of applying feng shui to your inner wealth while stimulating the finance center of your home at the same time.

Money is a form of energy. It must circulate in your life in order for you to materialize your dreams. Spiritual traditions have taught this for thousands of years, but it is a practical tool here and now. You may decide to donate a certain percentage of your income. Spread it out among charitable, life-saving, and spiritual organizations. Give to your parents, your children, and your employees. This concept is called tithing; you should give on a monthly basis. The aim is to give a portion of your income back in order for it to return. The concept originates from ancient times when farmers had to give one-tenth of their harvest back to the soil in order to grow a new crop. Give for the sake of giving and, at the same time, remember that this type of external giving is a vital ingredient in creating the future you desire. As you write the check or give the gift, decree silently that this tithe will come back to your and your family in the form of good health, happiness, and prosperity. You may also tithe for specific projects, goals, and for the success of others.

the positivity factor

The best advice is to use positive thinking every day. If your thoughts, words, and actions are full of positive energy, you will get positive results; remember, like attracts like. Have you noticed that the people who constantly complain about everything in their life continue to have bad luck? You have actually attracted that which surrounds you. In feng shui, when you fill your space with positive energy, it seeps into every aspect of your life.

Did you know that your subconscious takes orders from daily thoughts and words? It follows directions implicitly without asking questions. It manifests what you tell it day after day. You've heard the saying, "Be careful what you wish for, it may just come true." Well, it does, good or bad. So, make sure you are mindful of what you say. In *Your Infinite Power To Be Rich*, Dr. Joseph

Murphy maintains, "Your thoughts, mental imagery, beliefs, attitudes, and feelings are investments which you deposit in your subconscious mind. Your subconscious gives compound interest, i.e., it magnifies whatever you deposit. Impress your subconscious with love, faith, confidence, right action, guidance, abundance, security, and good humor, and whenever you need love, confidence, or an answer to a problem, your subconscious will supply you. This is the way to dig treasures out of the gold mine within you." Use the power of your subconscious to work for and not against you. Uplift yourself. It's in your power, not anyone else's.

tools for staying positive and energized

Over the years, my main goal has been searching for ways to lead a happier life. Here are some of my favorite techniques for staying plugged into a positive state of mind and health. I've tweaked them to work for me. Feel free to do the same. Family, friends, and clients use them every single day, as I do. Put them into practice. Share them with your loved ones, coworkers, and acquaintances. It's fun to help each other avoid negative thought patterns, people, or situations and to encourage the positive ones. Commit to the mindset that they will work! This is a basic ingredient in using feng shui in your life.

"A Story That Doesn't Need to Happen"

What do you do when a negative thought or series of thoughts come into your mind? How can you stop the scenario from unfolding? It is amazing how our minds start going down a negative path, picking up momentum. Then, all of a sudden, we are totally depressed, fearful, or anxious. You convince yourself this negative event is going to happen. For instance, imagine that you are driving to work for a very important meeting. You are going faster than usual because you are running late. Your mind wanders towards panicky thoughts of being pulled over by the police, getting a ticket, arriving late to work, losing your job, getting evicted from your house, living on the street, and on and on it goes. You have spiraled downward, and it's difficult to find your way back to reality. Perhaps the example is excessive, but many people engage in this type of thinking. Now is the time to stop, and here's a great method to help you accomplish it.

A simple story in Joel and Michelle Levey's book, *Living in Balance,* caught my eye. It involves a technique taken from a tribe in Africa, and it works wonders. They write, "From an early age, children there were trained to be mindful of their thinking. If a person became aware of a foreboding thought like, 'Oh no, what if there is a lion hiding behind that tree waiting to eat me?' They learned first to recognize and then release the thought by saying to themselves, 'This is a story that doesn't need to happen!'" That's the technique. You must say those exact words. If you start down a pessimistic road of thinking and the "what ifs" arise, stop, and say out loud, "That's a story that doesn't need to happen!" If your friends begin a similar conversation, recite the phrase to them, and encourage them to repeat it. You will feel a big difference by redirecting your thinking. Another simple way of terminating negative thoughts is by saying, "Erase, erase." Wave your hand in the air, side to side, as if you are actually erasing the thought from a schoolroom chalkboard. The idea is to interrupt your current state by a change of action or phrase. It really works. Stop taking yourself so seriously. Have fun staying positive.

The Energy Cord

One of the most useful techniques I learned from Master Choa Kok Sui is the idea of cutting the cord. Remember that there is an invisible cord connecting you to every person you interact with on a daily basis. Whether it's a partner, child, parent, boss, coworker, friend, or customer service representative, you are trading energy with them at every moment. Each encounter, in person or on the phone, will either energize or deplete you. Have you ever arrived at work feeling fantastic only to be bombarded by a colleague in a horrible mood? What happens to your energy? It constricts, and you want to stay as far away from them as possible. You actually might feel contaminated because their negative energy is polluting yours. What happens when a friend calls you up crying and in need of your support. You spend a half-hour comforting, talking, and encouraging. By the end of the conversation, you are exhausted and feel drained; however, your friend feels much better. What happened? Energy flows from high to low. You had more energy, and your friend was lucky enough to receive it. If you are at a job or in a family situation where many people come to you for support, you may be giving out too much of your precious life energy.

The easiest method to protect yourself and to keep your energy from draining away is to literally cut the cord. Do not be alarmed. You are only cutting the depleting cords and not the positive, nurturing ones. You should cut all of your cords before going to sleep at night. In this way, you will sleep without anyone depleting your energy, and you will awaken feeling refreshed. Feel free to cut the cord in the following situations:

From a bad day

From a negative person or situation

From your own negative thoughts

From an upsetting phone call

From the news on television or radio

From something that frightens you

From work (especially during the weekend or on vacation)

Here are some specifics to help you cut the cord.

- Imagine a cord extending from your solar plexus to the other person.
- Lift your arm up over your head and look at it. Pretend it's a purple samurai sword.
- Swing your arm down, crossing the front of your body, and imagine that you have just cut the cord between you and the person, event, or situation.
- Announce out loud, "I'm cutting the cord from (whomever or whatever)," as you make the sweeping movement with your arm.
- Repeat it as many times as you need to. You can also use shortcut words like "Cut, cut," "Snip, snip," "Bye-bye," or all three!

your energy investments

In *Why People Don't Heal and How They Can*, Caroline Myss explains that people have a "cellular bank account" where they store energy to power and heal the body. As an example, she asks you to imagine that one hundred circuits of energy pour into the top of your head every morning. These are deposited in your cellular bank account. She illustrates, "Imagine this flow of energy as a financial allowance equal to one hundred dollars per day. Your task is to learn how to invest this money wisely, because your investments will either earn you interest or

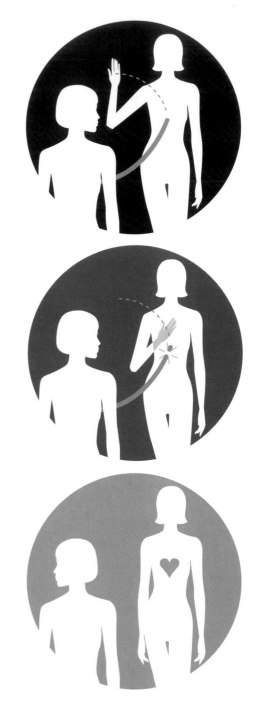

ABOVE: A simple way to increase your energy is to disconnect from negative people and situations by cutting the energy cord that connects you to them.

RIGHT: Use your precious energy to move forward in life by plugging into positive emotions and detaching from destructive ones.

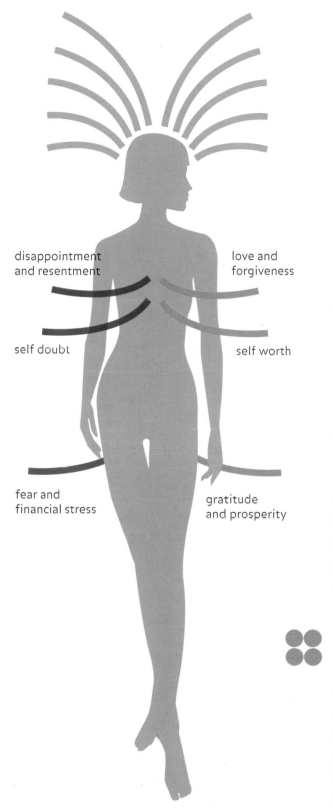

disappointment
and resentment

love and
forgiveness

self doubt

self worth

fear and
financial stress

gratitude
and prosperity

put you into debt." Thus, you are either energized or depleted, depending on where you allow your energy to go. Positive people and situations give you energy interest; the negative ones place you into energy debt.

Every day, you should investigate where and to whom your energy is going. How much energy do you want to give away, and how much do you want to invest in your health, success, and creative endeavors? Since you only have a hundred units, you need to plug into the right people and situations. If you notice your energy going towards a negative thought, person, or circumstance, tell yourself to "detach." Imagine that your energy circuits are detaching, coming back, and plugging into your own body. Visualize your aura full of one million energy dollars; be thankful you are compounding energetic interest!

Keeping good company increases your overall health and success. Don't let negative folks bring you down. Apply the concept of spring-cleaning to the people and situations that do not encourage you to live with enthusiasm. The more positive and successful you are, the more you will attract like-minded people into your life. As you apply feng shui principles to your home, you will be urged to surround yourself with positive energy in the form of physical objects such as inspiring books, enchanting music, photos with smiling faces, and cherished mementos. Create the same feeling in your relationships.

attitude of gratitude

Cultivating an attitude of gratitude keeps you in the present moment and soothes your soul. Look around you on a daily basis and notice all of the blessings in your life. Any time you feel blue, acknowledge the small things that make you happy. Be grateful for the food you eat, a sunny day, a warm bed, a healthy body, the ability to smell flowers, a tender

hug, a playful moment with your pet, and laughter with your family. Avoid concentrating on what is wrong and what you don't have. Let go of judgment and small irritations. Focus on the good parts when times get tough, on abundance rather than lack. Appreciate the beautiful moments. Your brain will shift gears, your heart will open, and the energy will begin to flow.

tools to encourage gratitude

- Keep a gratitude journal. Write in it every night before bed. List five to ten reasons you are grateful for the day. You can always begin with "I am grateful I am breathing."
- Spoil yourself with small gifts that you can be thankful for at the end of the day. Take a bath, buy raspberries for your cereal, play poker with the guys, get the car washed, sit in the sun, or plan a romantic dinner with your companion.
- Take a walk in a park, on the beach, in the mountains, or in your neighborhood, and literally point out all of the little things you are thankful you can see, hear, touch, or taste.
- At dinner, give thanks for the food and all your blessings. Tell loved ones everything that you love and appreciate about them.

the importance of clear intention

In feng shui, the energy of your home can be directed towards your unique goals and aspirations. Energy follows thought. What does that mean exactly? It means with strong intention, your thoughts can manifest physically. Make it a daily practice to visualize your outcomes and watch them begin to take shape. Directing your attention and will towards a thought repeatedly activates an energy force to make it happen.

For example, before you build a house, it begins as an idea in your head. It is in an invisible energy form. Whatever occurs in the physical world starts out in the energy world. The energy becomes denser as you take action. You get excited as you look at homes, flip through magazines, and hire an architect to convert your ideas into blueprints. The blueprints serve as the map to your

LEFT: Sharing a picnic of abundant, delectable foods is a great way to connect and laugh with friends and family, and experience gratitude towards them.

dream house. From there, people are hired to construct the home, apply the paint, landscape the garden, and decorate the interior. The house materializes from a vision in your head.

In the same way, if you want to have a healthy, loving, and abundant life, you must design a detailed and impeccable energy blueprint. Using feng shui in your home gives you the opportunity to create the blueprint for success around you, creating a higher probability of life to unfold in a way you desire. You must supply your home with the correct energy for it to support you in moving in the right direction.

your map to success

The law of manifestation tells us that a thought you hold repeatedly with conviction tends to manifest. The stronger your intention, the faster your goals will materialize. If you don't know where you are going, you'll have a hard time getting there. Your intention is your compass. Equate it to an outline for a term paper. Better yet, equate it to this book. Before each chapter, I wrote a detailed outline explaining all of the important information that I wished to convey. Once I determined the specifics, I could successfully envision the outcome of the book. I knew where I was going. With the outline in front of me, I asked for guidance. I requested that the feng shui faucet be turned on. Energy soon began to flow through me. I wrote every day. The chapters manifested because I followed a detailed outline, yet I allowed creativity to take its rightful course. Sometimes, it manifested in a new and wonderful way that I never could have imagined.

As you create your road map, you will be outlining what you want in your life. You will be planting the seeds for your future in your surroundings. Let the seeds germinate. Do not dig them up every two minutes to see if they have grown yet. If your intention is strong, if you use feng shui techniques, and if you actively participate in creating your goal, you will achieve results. However, try to avoid anticipating how something will manifest. You may be completely surprised as to how or when it comes into being. You and the energy of your home are unique, and energy materializes in different ways for each person. Your karma, destiny, and life path are special. No two manifestations will be alike. Just have faith and follow directions. The ways of the universe and energy are mysterious and dynamic – let them do their work.

your goals

Feng shui involves two main ingredients. First, you are responsible for supplying the correct type and amount of energy to your environment; the energy is like fuel for a car. Second, you must be purposeful about where you put your attention. Attention involves focusing. You must place what you want to create in the foreground of your mind. By placing your dreams, goals, and desires in full view within your environment, you are forced to focus on them rather than on a blank or negative canvas. In essence, you will be painting your own picture of happiness and success and placing yourself at the center of the picture.

Writing your goals forces you to be clear. The clearer your intention, the faster it will manifest. Throughout the rest of the book, you will actively and purposefully use the tools of feng shui to create the life you desire. As discussed, you need a road map to know where to start and what your destination is. You have your own unique desires for your space and life. Here is where you can concentrate on the specifics. Some of you want to remove the clutter from your home; others want to attract a relationship; some may simply want to decorate with a feng shui style.

Your Feng Shui Journal

To begin, choose a blank book to use as your feng shui journal. Write your answers to the following questions and make notes as you apply feng shui principles to your space. Bring your journal with you on shopping expeditions. Keep your entire feng shui experience in one place so you can refer back to it repeatedly. Writing down where you are now and where you want to be will give you an understanding of how far you have come. You can look back in six months to see what materialized and to give yourself a giant pat on the back. The following are questions to help you understand what is working in your life and what you would like to change or enhance. Let energy flow through you; write to your heart's content.

Overview Questions

What do you love about your home, room by room?

What do you dislike about your home, room by room?

How do you feel when you walk through your front door?

Does your home have an abundance of natural light or is it dark and gloomy?

Is your home in good repair?

Do you have clutter that depletes you the moment you see it?

Do you feel comfortable inviting friends and colleagues into your home or do you generally opt to meet elsewhere?

How much of the contents of your home have been chosen by you? How much is inherited? Are there hand-me-downs? Are you displaying objects from a past relationship?

Do you like being at home or would you rather stay away?

Do you feel motivated and full of potential when you are at home?

Do your home and office symbolize who you really are and where you hope to go?

take action now

Do not underestimate the power of these simple techniques. They work, so start simple. Select at least one technique and use it for a month. As you feel a change, you will be inspired to use more techniques. Trick yourself by doing one that only takes five minutes. New actions lead to new behaviors, which lead to new life.

1. **get your journal** and answer all of these questions. Write early in the morning when you are rested and ready for change.

2. **create good karma** by giving to a charity, your spiritual organization, or your employees once a month. Sponsor a needy child. Offer your time to a homeless shelter, send money to the Red Cross, give to a food drive, or plant a tree. Give for the sake of giving and remember, when you give you also receive.

3. **absorb tree energy** by sitting on the grass barefoot and asking a tree for its excess energy. Be aware of the life force around you and ask for guidance. Breathe and meditate. Feel nature's flow. Smile.

4. **Send pink light.** Imagine you are sending a cloud of cotton candy from your heart to someone you love, to someone you wish to forgive, or to someone who needs healing.

5. **Start a gratitude journal.** Write every night before bed. Gratitude can be as simple as "Thanks for the warm sun today."

6. **Give a heart center rub.** Rub the front and back heart areas of a friend or loved one. You can also touch your own heart center to remind you to be kind to yourself.

Life Questions

Are you living out your passions? If not, can you identify them?

Is your love life fulfilling? How could it be even more enjoyable?

Is your health good or would you like to improve it?

How is your career? What are your goals?

Are you expressing your creativity?

What new aspects of life would you like to discover?

Are there books or classes that would stimulate your passion?

Are you happy with your reputation personally and professionally?

Are your finances abundant?

How are your relationships with family, children, friends, and colleagues?

How do you feel about your connection with your soul and spirit? Do you have a space where you can be quiet, feel centered, and ask for guidance?

Are you in harmony with the other people living in your home?

Focus Questions

What is most important in your life right now?

What is least important?

In order of importance, list the ten aspects you would like to focus on enhancing in your life right now.

Congratulations! You are already much closer to realizing your dreams. This is an important step in turning your undivided attention towards your goals. The more you dive into the infinite possibilities in your life, the faster they will take material form. I hope this writing exercise has helped you discover your unique goals, dreams, and aspirations

joyful living

Embrace a life full of gratitude, love, harmony, joy, and passion. You can feng shui your spirit by incorporating the acts in the list below into daily living. Make a copy of this list and keep it on the fridge, or somewhere in the house where you're likely to see it regularly. Let it remind you to take good care of your body and soul each day of your life.

Expect grace in every moment.

Become a force for good.

Write down your blessings.

Laugh, giggle, and be goofy.

Pray or meditate as a daily ritual.

Trust your instincts.

Create alone time to just "be."

Eat scrumptious and healthy foods.

Plan a dream vacation – a dream life.

Keep good company.

Breathe slowly and deeply.

Sit quietly under a tree.

Skip down the road.

Go barefoot in the soft grass.

Swim in the sea.

Plant a colorful, sweet-smelling garden.

Don't rush!

Relax into a great book.

Take a soothing salt bath.

Be silent.

Stay present.

Ask for guidance.

Listen to the whisperings of your soul.

Follow your dreams.

Smile.

Make extraordinary decisions.

Visualize your outcomes.

Soak up nature's healing energy.

Rejuvenate your body with loads of water.

Cherish your family and friends.

Honor and express your feelings.

Let go of expectations.

Create boundaries and be honest.

Forgive yourself and others.

Don't take things personally.

Try being loving instead of being right.

Remember happy times with happy pictures.

Worry less, play more, and play big.

Stay positive and have faith.

Step out and take a risk.

Summon childlike enthusiasm.

Move your body...dance and sing!

Explore new situations and opportunities.

See beauty everywhere you go.

Make a spiritual pilgrimage.

Create a cycle of giving and receiving.

Delight in small miracles.

Let your spirit fly.

three:
clutter and space cleansing

Clearing clutter and cleansing space are the first steps in creating awesome energy within yourself and your surroundings. Just as an artist paints a masterpiece on a fresh canvas, a clean environment is essential for you to implement feng shui effectively. If you start with a clean slate, your dreams and goals will manifest much faster and easier.

As you paint your destiny around you, it's important not to let your past weigh down the brush and disrupt the flow. Removing physical, emotional, and energy debris is a major component of feng shui. In your body, your blood circulates freely when there are no obstructions. Similarly, as you remove clutter, energy pours through you and creates a fertile environment for opportunities to take hold.

Suppose you want to restore a cherished old desk. Compare the steps you take to revive the desk with the process of creating good feng shui. First, you must strip the old paint. Second, you sand the desk to make it smooth. Third, you apply primer to prepare the wood surface. Finally, you paint it the color you desire. Visualize incorporating feng shui in the same way. Clearing clutter is similar to stripping the paint. It cleans away all of the old, excess stuff. Organizing your environment is like sanding. It produces a smooth system on which to build. Cleansing the space of negative energies corresponds to applying the primer. It creates a pure environment for positive energy to adhere easily and last longer. Finally, painting the desk is like implementing feng shui enhancements. Finishing each step ensures the success of the final result.

Get excited about the clearing process. Tap into the vision of the unlimited possibilities that await you on the other side of chaos. It is important to start small and build your clutter-clearing muscle in a balanced way. Take it one step at a time. You are close to realizing your potential; activate your will and creativity to keep you focused on your outcome.

clutter

Clutter comes in all shapes and sizes. In the thesaurus, the synonyms for clutter are mess, pile, heap, hodgepodge, jumble, tangle, disorder, disarray, confusion, and chaos. Your clutter may be stacked in corners, piled on tables, stuffed in drawers, squished in filing cabinets, packed in attics, and hidden behind closed doors. Unfortunately, wherever it materializes, you feel depleted just thinking about it. In feng shui terms, clutter creates stagnant energy that keeps you trapped in every way imaginable. The motto, "Healthy energy is moving energy," applies here. If you cannot move through your home without being obstructed by clutter, you can be

ABOVE: The foyer should be bright and uncluttered so positive energy can easily pass through and circulate into the rest of the home.

certain that subtle energy will not be able to flow either. When energy stops flowing, life stops progressing.

Clutter has ramifications beyond impeding your progress in your physical space. It also affects your emotional, mental, and energetic health. If your space is cluttered, you may feel inundated with unrelated emotional issues. If your head is cluttered with all of your unfinished tasks, organizing your space is the last thing on your mind. Energetically, clutter pulls the vibrant energy of the environment down and instigates a heavy sigh of exhaustion. When your inside and outside worlds are cluttered simultaneously, you find it nearly impossible to envision actualizing your dreams. Enormous amounts of healthy, creative energy will pour into your life as you take the reins and become the master of your domain.

types of clutter

The four kinds of clutter keep you from moving forward in your personal and professional life.

Common Clutter

You have too much unused, unloved, unnecessary, and messy stuff littering your space. Examples include junk mail, broken objects, old newspapers, and magazines.

Symbolic Clutter

You have objects that consciously or unconsciously affect your emotions and thoughts in a negative way. Examples include unsuccessful projects, gloomy artwork, and disheartening books.

Energy Clutter

All items are attached to you by an invisible cord. Some instantaneously deplete your energy. Examples include photos of people who disapprove of you, gifts from a past relationship, and inherited furniture you've kept out of guilt.

Mental and Emotional Clutter

These are unresolved emotional issues, tasks you've avoided handling, and draining relationships. Examples are friends you need to confront, doctor's appointments to be scheduled, and people you need to clear from your life.

ABOVE: Organizing and color-coordinating your dinnerware is visually pleasing and allows you to locate items faster.

the importance of a clutter-free life

Clutter affects your whole life. You cannot be successful in the way you have dreamed of if you are stuck in the quicksand of clutter. It keeps you lodged in the past. Clutter creates a feeling of pandemonium as you find yourself running in twenty directions simultaneously. With so many stimuli encircling you, it's impossible to focus on what to do, where to go, or what you want. How do you expect to achieve your goals if you are consumed with locating basic necessities amidst your chaos?

Feeling out of control in your environment seeps into your everyday life. Clutter pulls your energy down. You may experience this as feeling overwhelmed, exhausted, frustrated, confused, or depressed. Massive success and fulfillment do not fit into this equation. In some cases, your social life is negatively affected. You become so embarrassed by all your "stuff" that you avoid entertaining friends. If they do come by and it's a mess, what does that imply about who you are and how you feel about yourself? Turn the situation around.

Each time you enter a home or office, you make judgments instantaneously. People react the same towards you. You are in control of how people perceive you because you control how you care for yourself and your belongings. Set an impressive example of how you expect others to treat you by respecting yourself. A clean, orderly, and beautiful environment will establish a high standard.

Organizing your belongings will bring you liberation and expansion. Instead of focusing on what you are getting rid of, concentrate on moving towards your dream and goals. As soon as you begin, you will feel lighter, happier, more motivated, and more confident about yourself. When you remove the clutter, you'll have nothing holding you back, and your life will be free to take the form you envision for it.

Just clearing one drawer can open up your heart and mind to new possibilities. You will immediately feel a sense of relief and will have more energy to continue the process. Cut the cord to things that keep you stuck in the past. "Unplug" yourself from the turmoil in your environment so you can surge forward. You'll find that you are even clearer about your purpose because you've kept only those objects that encourage and inspire you. Susan Jeffers wrote a book with a wonderful title, *Feel the Fear and Do It Anyway*. When you feel uncertain, overwhelmed, or scared about clearing your clutter, recite that phrase over and over again. I do, and it helps. Remind yourself that the clearing process may not always feel comfortable, but it is essential to achieving harmony and success. Change isn't always easy, but the reward is nothing short of a personal evolution.

the way to good feng shui

Clearing clutter has a direct impact on how fast feng shui manifests in your surroundings. Your preparation guides energy to do its job more easily. Imagine you want to hike to the top of a mountain. Would you get there faster with a proper trail or without one? Finding your way through bushes, trees, rocks, and streams is more arduous than following a well-defined path. Think of clearing each piece of clutter as creating an open path for energy to move through. As you eliminate clutter, your goals will come into clear view.

From a feng shui standpoint, it is important to embark on clutter clearing with the following elements in mind.

Spring-cleaning

Rule number one is to "clean before you energize." It's important to sweep, wash, dust, and scrub the physical grime out of your environment. Open the windows to let in fresh air and sunshine. If your house is dirty, the energy circulating is dirty. So, clean, clean, clean.

Symbols

The symbols in your home are an important aspect in feng shui. What is your house saying to you and about you? Does each item you own represent who you are and where you want to go? Does each item have positive or negative attributes? What are the symbols surrounding you? Do they contribute to an optimistic outlook about your life?

Energy Attachment

As discussed previously, you are attached to every item you own by an invisible cord. Each piece either nourishes or depletes you. Each one retains the energy and memory of how and where you acquired it, the person that gave it to you, or the previous owner. As you scan your home, think about how these items affect you on a daily basis. You might ask yourself, "Which objects bring me joy and warmth? Which items upset, annoy, depress, infuriate, or frustrate me?"

Creating a Vacuum

This term suggests that you are opening up a physical and emotional space for new things to come into your life. Your intention in letting go of clutter

RIGHT: Daily confidence and efficiency begin with an orderly closet. Experience a surge of energy after ridding your closet of old, unworn, and undesirable clothes; replace old clothes with new ones that make you feel great.

is to bring in more abundance, opportunities, and blessings. You may attract a new love, car, or job. The idea is to make room for fresh prospects. Creating a vacuum, internally and externally, attracts good fortune.

Treat yourself lovingly and give yourself the gift of a clutter-free existence. Your eyes deserve a beautiful view. You might need to clear it every week, month, or six months. Just as a gardener comes once a week to ensure your plants are trimmed and your flowers are blooming, you must be the gardener of your space. Weed when necessary and plant seeds of beauty all around you.

reasons for clutter

Clutter builds up for numerous reasons. Sometimes it is the result of external problems within your home. For instance, storage space is limited, you have too much stuff, or you haven't established an easy-to-use organizational system. The problem may occur because your spouse, child, or roommate cannot control their clutter. However, emotional or psychological obstacles can also cause an inability to let go and clean up. You may be sabotaging yourself on a subconscious level.

Unbeknownst to you, clutter might be serving a deeper purpose. You may be hiding behind it out of fear of failure or success. If you are afraid of intimacy, clutter might be an excellent excuse to keep people at a distance. Perhaps you think that your creativity arises out of the confusion and that you need the clutter to produce results. Fear seems to be the common denominator. If you can identify why you are holding on to clutter, you'll have an easier time making informed decisions about whether to keep things or to get rid of them. The inability to let go is a product of fear. This leads to immobilization and stagnancy. When space is cluttered, energy comes to a standstill. Since feng shui is predicated on energy circulation, you must clear it to get the ball rolling.

emotional reasons
People hold on to clutter for a number of emotional reasons.

"Just in Case"

You may be holding on to items because "you never know when you might need them." If you have experienced lean times in your life, you may fill your need for security by keeping an abundance of things around you. You are afraid to relinquish items that are familiar to you. This "just in case" mentality generates a feeling that something is lacking rather than a feeling of abundance. Examples of "just in case" items are broken appliances to be repaired later, old clothes and shoes, and ten-year-old financial papers. Almost everything stored in the garage, including inoperable cars, bicycles, and electronic equipment fits into this category. Each item you keep "just in case" further roots you in fear and lack. Be confident that you will have everything you need and want to lead a happy life. An effective way to start a cycle of abundance is by giving away items that no longer serve you. As you give, you receive. Create a vacuum for new and wonderful things to enter your home.

Past Associations

You may have a sentimental attachment to certain objects in your home. There are two points to consider in this case. First, it is important to recognize if the attachment serves you. Second, if it makes you happy, is it absolutely necessary to display it? If you have a collection of your favorite grandmother's china, then it is probably a positive association. However, you may be holding on to items from past relationships and events that negatively affect your emotions on a daily basis. Objects from an unsuccessful relationship, uniforms from past employment, and pictures of people who didn't support you fall into this category. If an object makes you sad or keeps your attention in the past, you might want to consider putting it away.

You have a limited amount of space and you want to fill it with special objects that bring you joy. Perhaps you have items you bought during a wonderful time in your life. For instance, you have a closet full of clothes from five years ago when you were twenty pounds lighter. You are afraid to get rid of them even though you don't wear them. Perhaps you feel you will forget those "thin" moments. However, every time you see them, you feel bad that you haven't lost the weight. Ask yourself if you want to focus on the past or concentrate on your future. The answer varies for each person, and it depends on how much clutter you have weighing you down. If the item anchors you to an incredibly successful memory, you may decide to keep it. Use your intuition.

Guilt

How many items do you keep in your home because you genuinely love them? What percentage of your belongings have you inherited or been given? Are you displaying them out of guilt? You may be holding onto objects because you feel that you should. It's time to take control of your space. Just because somebody gives you a gift doesn't mean that you have to like it or to display it. You are not showing a lack of respect for them or loving them any less if you decide to put it away because it's not your taste.

Every time you look at the sweater your best friend bought you that isn't your style, you feel guilty for not wearing it. Or perhaps you inherited a picture that your father painted. You feel indebted to him and even though you don't like it, you hang it up. The problem is that you wince every time you see it, which depletes your energy. The solution is to take it down, store it, or give it to someone who will love it. If your parents visit once a year, you can always hang it back up for that short period of time. The same applies to every book, candle, vase, painting, and artifact that has been given to you. If it doesn't make you happy, let it go or, at the very least, put it away for a while.

Inherited Clutter Habits

If you come from a long line of clutter bugs, you may be carrying on the tradition. Usually, if your parents lived with clutter, you learned to do the same. Sometimes, no matter how hard you try to beat the habit, your mom comes by with another box of great old stuff she would love you to have. If your parents lived through the depression or World War II, they learned to keep things "just in case." There were extreme shortages, and times were hard. They felt they had to hold on to everything for good reason. It might have been a reality for your parents back then, but it is probably not so for you today. You may find yourself collecting items at garage sales, flea markets, and bargain stores in order to surround yourself with as much stuff as your parents had. They bought in bulk; now, you do. Their anxiety has turned into yours. Break the pattern for yourself and your children. Teach your kids to detach from "things," and allow them to grow up in a home that emanates a feeling of abundance.

physical clutter

Various categories of clutter accumulate in different areas of the home and office. In chapter five, you will find that your clutter may be located in the middle of your Wealth, Health, or Love center, making it difficult for energy to circulate in those precious spots. Clutter residing in those places will slow down your wealth, health, and love potential. As you read through this section, walk around your space making notes of where most of your clutter lies. Identify the kinds of clutter you have and why you have it. Using your intuition, look at each piece of clutter.

Consider whether it represents you in the present or in the past. Does it increase or deplete your energy? In the next section, you will learn techniques to help you clear it.

messy papers

Where to look for it: Dining room, living room, kitchen, bedroom, office, and car.

What to look for: Papers, junk mail, newspapers, magazines, bills, coupons, receipts, phone messages, take-out menus, old files, financial statements, business cards, college notebooks, and birthday and holiday cards from the last twenty years.

What to do with it: Throw it out, recycle it, or organize it.

things you don't use or wear

Where to look for it: Kitchen cabinets, bathrooms, bedrooms, closets, attic, basement, garage, under the bed, and behind doors.

What to look for: Expired foods, old pots and pans, mangled plastic containers, expired or unused bath products, make-up and cologne, broken electronics, appliances, furniture, rusty tools, storage boxes, things you haven't worn in a year, shoes that don't fit or have holes, broken holiday ornaments, anything

conquering clutter

If you feel overwhelmed about clearing clutter, the following is a good mental tool that might help you to subdue it. In fact, feel free to use it with any problem you might have. In feng shui, one of the goals is to reprogram your house to bring in good fortune. In the same way, it is important to redirect your thought processes to be successful. When you have problems or fears, you usually visualize them as much larger than yourself. You may say you are "fighting your inner demons," or you may feel as if a tidal wave is about to drown you. When you consider problems in this overpowering manner, it seems impossible to conquer them. How can you triumph over your fears when, in your head, you are pint-sized and they seem monstrous? The trick is to imagine your problem or fear as a pesky little fly that you can effortlessly flick away. This will allow you to view the problem as annoying but minor. It will not consume you. Practice this visualization over and over again. Each time, you will feel stronger and more capable. Do not let your clutter conquer you!

you don't like, and old, stained, and ripped clothing.

What to do with it: Throw it out, donate it, or repair it.

collections of things

Where to look for it: Living room, dining room, bedrooms, garage, attic, and office.

What to look for: Books, photos, antiques, record albums, stamps, baseball cards, animal statues, items you had a fetish for in the past and still own, anything that you own more than ten of.

What to do with it: Donate it, minimize it, or organize it in a contained space.

things that drain your energy

Where to look for it: Everywhere.

What to look for: Objects that remind you of a negative person or event, gifts you never liked, objects that are no longer "you," items with negative symbolism, and inherited items you have kept out of guilt.

What to do with it: Give it to friends, throw it out, or donate it.

the first steps

First and foremost, take the clearing process lightly and make it fun. It's not always going to be your favorite activity, so pair it up with something that puts a swing in your step. Infuse energy into the space by playing upbeat music and opening the windows. Try not to get distracted by phone calls or other projects that could cause you to lose your momentum. You need to establish a good rhythm.

Set a specific amount of time and a particular area you would like to clear. You will feel good about yourself if you stay on track. Keep your mind on all of the positive reasons why you are removing clutter. Focus on new things, opportunities, more space, and time to do what you are truly passionate about. At the end of each session, write down your accomplishments and decide how to give yourself a treat for a job well done. Depending on your taste, you may want to get a massage, go out for a delicious meal, play golf, or simply take a walk at sunset.

Try to remember that clearing clutter is not life or death. If by some chance, you get rid of an item you wish you had kept, you may miss it, but it will not ruin your life. Don't spend too long on any single item. If you cannot make up your mind, place it in a "not sure" box and keep moving. At the end of the session, go back to the box. If you still can't make a firm decision about a particular item, store it for a month or two. Notice if you miss it or need it. If you don't, then you can let it go for good.

In transforming the energy of your home, keep only the items you love. Let go in small ways. Open a space for change to take place. You should create clear and empty areas for your eyes to rest on. This will give you clarity to discover what you want in the present.

Negotiate with others living in your home. If one person likes a particular item and you do not, ask them to keep it in their personal area of the house. In this way, you do not have to look at it all of the time. What one person loves, another might detest. You must respect others' belongings but do not allow them to control you or your space. Explain to all inhabitants that you are clearing clutter to uplift the energy of the entire house, including theirs. Ask them to help keep clutter to a minimum. Obviously, the job is a lot easier if everyone is in agreement and desires the same result.

clutter-clearing questions

Asking yourself the right questions will help you decide if each item is encouraging good feng shui or counteracting it. Many times your first instinct is the right one. Your goal is to keep only those items that support a vibrant, harmonious, and successful life. Answer these questions honestly to help you clear the clutter.

- Do I love it?
- Do I use it?
- Do I need it?
- Does it evoke a positive feeling and make me smile?

clearing bags or boxes

Depending on what is easiest for you, buy boxes or large trash bags to facilitate the organization process. Label each one with a colored note. Use the following list as a model. Feel free to customize it to work for you.

- **Trash**—Garbage of any sort

- **Recycle**—Papers, newspapers, magazines, plastics, and glass bottles
- **Donate**—Items in good condition but no longer needed, such as old clothes, appliances, books, shoes, etc.
- **Filing**—Unorganized financial and personal papers
- **Future Gifts**—Items given to you that are not your style
- **Not Sure**—Items you don't know if you want to keep
- **Storage**—Items you would like to keep but do not want displayed or kept inside the home

scheduling time

Schedule time in your calendar to clear out the clutter. Using your free time does not work. You will end up making other plans that you consider more enjoyable. Once you have figured out how many cluttered areas you want to clear, you must designate a specific period of time for each of them. After you establish momentum, you will be able to gauge how long it will take. Be realistic and give yourself breaks. Plan fun outings around your sessions so you have something to look forward to. When you finish a session, schedule your next one. Prepare your home for your wishes to become realities.

two people are better than one

Removing clutter moves faster with four hands than with two hands. Enlist a professional or ask a friend to assist you. Ask someone who has no personal investment in your items to help you make decisions. If you have the money, you may want to hire a professional organizer. They will have their own system, and you may feel more secure having an expert in the house. You can find one in the classified advertisements of your local paper or on the Internet. Make sure to ask for referrals in order to choose one who will fit your needs.

Another option is to ask a friend who is a wonderful organizer to help you. You may want to reciprocate in some way. Treat them to dinner or a concert. You might offer your time

---

tips for starting the clearing process

- **Try easy things first**—Start with the "no-brainers." This includes old newspapers, magazines, trash, junk mail, coupons, expired foods and prescriptions, outdated schedules, broken items, and old cans of paint. Take special care to clear clutter from behind doors and under your bed.
- **Start small and build momentum**—Begin in a simple area before graduating to larger ones. Trick yourself into clearing one shelf or counter that won't take too much time. Once you conquer a small area, you will have more energy, and you will be inspired to move on.
- **Tackle visible areas**—Clean out the visible areas before conquering the hidden areas like drawers, cabinets, and closets. Seeing tangible results will motivate you to keep going. Begin with tabletops, counters, bookcases, desk surfaces, and the floor.
- **Complete one area at a time**—Sometimes, when you begin the clearing process, you start with your desk, move to a bookshelf, and then to the bedroom all in the same hour. You keep finding objects that need to be organized in another location. Do not go back and forth between areas. You end up scattering your energy and wasting time. You won't see results anywhere.
- **Clean up after each session**—Place all garbage bags in the trash or take them to the dump. Place donation bags, dry cleaning, and objects to be repaired in your trunk so that you can drop them off. Tidy up the area in which you have worked so you feel that you have made progress.

and talent to assist them in some project. Paint a picture, give a massage, or prepare their taxes. Maybe you have a buddy who also needs some organizing, and you can trade off each weekend, that would be beneficial for both of you.

Your friend can support you both emotionally and physically. On the emotional level, another person is invaluable because your assistant is not attached to your belongings. Your helper can ask you critical questions: "Do you love it?" "Do you really need it?" On a physical level, your helper can hold each item up for inspection so you can determine the appropriate bag or box for it. Once you develop momentum, clearing becomes fun. Bring out the dust mop and a wet rag to clean up each area. Crank up the music and drink loads of water so that you don't become dehydrated.

the beginning

Establishing a system where every object has its proper place is essential in order to create a clutter-free environment. Simplify and organize.

ABOVE: Start clearing clutter by removing excess books, magazines, and bills from your night table and putting inspiring art, fresh flowers, and a journal in their place.

You may need to add extra storage units including shelving, filing cabinets, storage containers, and bookshelves. Line the walls of your garage and basement with floor-to-ceiling shelving. Inside your home, hang ornamental doors or colorful curtains to cover existing bookshelves and cabinets. Drape a scarf over a black metal filing cabinet or add doors to an entertainment center in order to hide videotapes and CDs. From a feng shui perspective, the more beautiful and harmonious the view, the better the space is for you.

Many times your paper clutter accumulates because the storage unit is too far from where you deal with your papers. For example, if you pay bills, work on the computer, and write notes in your dining room, a filing cabinet should be nearby. When the filing cabinet is in the office at the other end of the house, you are more apt to postpone filing your papers. Inevitably, the papers pile up on the table, disturbing a relaxed dining experience. Before filing, you may wish to organize current papers in four appealing boxes or baskets. Go through and clear them out at least once a month. Label the boxes:

Bills/Financial Papers
Personal
Career/Business
Family Engagements.

basements, attics, and garages

Don't fool yourself by shoving your excess stuff in the attic, basement, or garage. Energy must flow in every area of your house including the unseen, utilitarian spaces. Each room attached to your home counts. The attic represents your higher aspirations. If clutter is looming over your head, you may be stopping the flow of guidance coming in to inspire you. Your mental and spiritual faculties might feel blocked. Basements represent the emotions that you push down because you don't want to deal with them. The basement also symbolizes your grounding. Healthy, fertile soil beneath you encourages your goals, dreams, and aspirations to grow and prosper. Many times the garage is the first view you have when you come home and the last you see before starting your day. If you drive in and out of clutter every day, your energy will be constantly drained. You feel guilty about the mess and swear you will clean it up each weekend. You end up spending more energy

ABOVE: Make sure your pantry has ample shelving to help you easily locate different foods and supplies. Label each shelf to encourage the entire household to participate in unpacking groceries and preparing meals.

happy photos

Photographs should be cleaned out and organized in boxes or albums. Throw out pictures that you feel are not flattering or in which part of your body is cut off. Also discard photos taken at times when you were not happy. No rule dictates that you must treasure every picture you take. Do not keep copies or pictures that do not elicit a positive response. If you want to bring in new love, take down photos displaying past partners.

Replace the pictures you've removed with those of new friends, recent vacations, and joyful family occasions. Be sure to place these in attractive frames. As you organize your photos, enlarge new ones to replace old baby pictures, graduations, and other such events. Choose one with a new pose, background, people, or color. When you have seen the same photos around your house for many years, you may not even notice them anymore. Add new stimuli and fresh energy to your environment. Surround yourself with happy memories and uplifting people.

stressing about the clutter than you would expend in clearing it. If you still have unopened boxes from the last move, five or ten years ago, my bet is that you have no idea what is inside of them, and you probably don't need anything in them. Store items you want to keep but do not need daily in an off-site storage unit, so they will not affect you in your home. Organize each storage area in your home. You will feel like a new person.

designate a home

Every item needs a place to "live." In order for you to find what you need quickly and easily, assign your objects a permanent home. Create a specific area for items to reside; they will not magically organize themselves. This is how clutter piles up. When possible, use containers to group similar items such as spices, make-up, jewelry, first-aid items, office supplies, toys, photos, videotapes, board games, wrapping paper, cleaning supplies, camping gear, and tools. Use labels so everyone in the house will be able to find them and replace them. Call a meeting to show everyone where each item now lives.

In general, look around the house to find areas that seem to invite clutter. Place a storage unit close by. If you work on creative projects in the living room, keep a decorative storage box within reach. An antique chest or trunk provides good storage for living rooms, dens, and bedrooms. If you read your mail in the kitchen, designate a drawer for bills, invitations, and other papers. If you read books and magazines by the fireplace, a wicker basket or magazine rack close by will organize them in one spot.

The crucial point is to keep clutter from accumulating on the floor. This is a serious feng shui no-no. When it happens, energy collects on the ground, causing you to feel depleted. Energy must always go up. Think "high" rather than "low." Uplifting, heightening, raising, and elevating energy in yourself and your surroundings is the essence of applying feng shui to your life.

emotional and mental clutter

Clear out the nooks and crannies of your heart and mind. Just as physical clutter affects you, so do your worries, upsets, and frustrations. Your emotions and thoughts become clogged. You will have more energy available to create your future if you clean the inner and outer simultaneously. If you let go of a draining relationship, you will usually have more energy to give to your house. In the same way, when you clean your space, the energy pouring in will enable you to manifest a healthy relationship. Clearing all types of clutter will bring harmony to your heart, mind, and surroundings.

Emotional clutter represents unexpressed feelings in your heart as well as negative people in your life. When you do not communicate honestly with loved ones, colleagues, and friends, your emotions become blocked and confused. You must express your feelings, thoughts, wants, needs, and boundaries. Writing in a journal can give you clarity. You get hurt when you assume that others should know what you are feeling. Communicating is your responsibility. When you ask for what you want, you will have a much greater chance of receiving it. However, if certain people continually drain your energy, you might need to stop interacting with them. Clear out friends, companions, and colleagues if they do not contribute to your well-being.

Mental clutter encompasses all of the tasks that you put off dealing with. You have a difficult time handling your daily activities if you are bogged down with your unfinished chores. You must complete the tasks at hand to free your energy. Do not allow your errands to hang over your head. Prepare your taxes, respond to emails, get an oil change, drop off the dry cleaning, return phone calls, schedule appointments, and pay your bills.

Every time you think of the same twenty tasks, you lose energy. As you complete each one, cross it off your mental

collections

People collect items for various reasons. You may have inherited a collection of Civil War memorabilia, or started your own collection of dolls, model airplanes, tribal masks or albums by a particular band. Try to look at your collection objectively: Does it speak to your identity now, or does keeping it let the past "keep" you? Do these items hog space that new belongings, more appropriate to your life now, could occupy? Pare down your collection, keeping only those items most dear to you. Consider giving away some things for others to enjoy.

list. Chunk the items together to save time and get faster results. For example, plan to run five errands in the same part of town or set aside two hours to return all phone calls and pay bills. When you have unfinished tasks in the back of your mind, it's impossible to enjoy precious moments with family and friends. Now is the time to get down to the exciting business of creating your destiny.

space cleansing

Space cleansing is the practice of cleaning your energy environment. After clearing clutter and physically cleaning your environment, you must remove the energy debris that has built up over time. The idea is to bring positive, healthy, and loving energy into your surroundings. Once you perform the cleansing, the energy of the space lifts, brightens, and circulates freely. Then, implementing feng shui becomes a breeze.

The energy debris can be a result of negative emotions, thoughts, occurrences, and stress that you have experienced in your space. Your house is like a sponge. Whatever transpires in your environment is absorbed into the walls, furniture, carpet, ceiling, and objects. Frequently, these negative energies accumulate in the corners and tucked away places. Visualize space cleansing as wiping away dust bunnies from the past.

In addition, feng shui suggests that the health, finances, success, and happiness of previous tenants can affect you in the present. If the last inhabitants experienced a divorce, illness, or financial loss, those energy patterns become imprinted in your environment. The previous occupants moved out, but their dust bunnies still exist. You have no way of knowing what happened in the past. Since you are constantly moving in and out of homes, apartments, condominiums, and offices, you should cleanse all spaces. This provides you with the peace of mind that you have seriously cut the cord from their experiences.

Space cleansing can also be applied to specific objects. Antiques are a good example. Many times, you have no idea where the antique previously resided. Since objects are impregnated with the energy of each owner and all that transpired around them, you could be affected without even knowing it. Become conscious about items purchased at thrift stores and garage sales.

On the other hand, when positive energy is infused in objects, they usually bring good luck. You may believe your marriage is blessed because you wear your grandmother's wedding ring. Perhaps you sign all financial documents with the same pen your millionaire grandfather used. In addition, spiritual energies can be sensed in objects such as sacred texts, clothing, jewelry, and artifacts owned by holy people. All in all, my suggestion is always to cleanse your objects for your own protection.

when should you space cleanse?
The following situations are appropriate times to space cleanse:

   After you remove clutter
   After an argument
   When you move into a new space
   When a roommate or companion moves out
   After an illness or death
   When you buy an antique or second-hand item
   Anytime you desire fresh energy for a new project
   Before implementing feng shui

how to cleanse a space
Here is a simple space-cleansing technique to perform on your home, office, or even on a specific object:

- Create a strong intention in your mind to clear the space in order to bring in vibrant, healthy energy.
- Clap your hands up and down in each corner and closet with the intention of breaking up stagnant energy. Clap until you feel that the invisible dust bunnies are gone. Move on to the next corner or object. When you finish clapping in your space, wash your hands with soap to keep the dirty energy from contaminating your body.

ABOVE: Be certain to expel old energy by space cleansing before moving into your new home. Vibrations embedded in the walls, rugs, and furniture—especially in antiques—can have positive or negative effect.

salt burning for intense purification

For more extensive cleansing, you can perform a salt burning. Because fire is involved, you need to be very careful and to follow the directions. Use this technique after an illness or death. Also use it when you move into a new home. The fire will cleanse your emotions at the same time.

You will need:
- Small disposable aluminum bread pan for each room you want to cleanse
- One large aluminum pan (turkey-size)
- Rock salt
- Rubbing alcohol

Instructions:
Place enough rock salt in the small pan to cover the bottom. Pour just enough rubbing alcohol over the salt to soak it. Place the small pan inside the larger one for protection. Take the pan to the room you want to cleanse. Make sure you disconnect the smoke alarm temporarily. Place the large pan with the small one inside it in the middle of the room. Clear everything away. Say, "Thank you for the complete disintegration of all negative energies, thoughts, and emotions from this room now." Light a match and carefully drop it inside the small pan. A fairly large flame will burn. Keep your eyes on the fire and have a towel in reach. When the fire burns out completely, throw the small pan in the trash. Keep the large pan for the next room. Start the process again by adding salt to another small pan. Immediately afterwards, open the doors and windows for at least an hour to refill your home with fresh energy. Wash your hands with soap and reconnect the smoke alarm. Remove the trash from your environment.

- Burn sandalwood incense or dried sage to disintegrate the negative energy in each room. (Buy incense from India, Japan or China as the energy is stronger.) Wave it counterclockwise in each corner, closet, and cabinet. You may also let one stick burn in each room. Say, "Thank you for the complete disintegration of all negative energies, thoughts, and emotions from this room now."

- After cleansing, always open windows and doors to allow fresh energy to enter.

- Burn a stick of rose incense to bring love and harmony into the environment.

- Light a scented candle to dedicate energy to your endeavors. Say your wish out loud. For example, "I am so grateful for all the love, harmony, and healthy energy pouring into my home right now."

- Imagine brilliant white light filling the whole space. Visualize your home or office as a shining star emanating light, positive energy and blessing to everyone who enters.

quick energy cleanse

Always remember that one of the fastest ways to clean a room or object is by burning sandalwood incense. The energy coming out of each stick has a strong cleansing effect on the environment. You can buy it on the Internet, spiritual bookstores, and many natural food markets. Don't leave home without it.

RIGHT: To cleanse a space quickly, burn a piece of sandalwood incense. An attractive and unique incense burner can enhance the ritual.

clear your own energy field

During the clutter clearing and space cleansing processes, your energy field may become filled with emotions, stress, past associations, and negative residue. You must clean your aura to replenish it with vibrant and joyful energy. You'll find it wonderfully soothing to take a salt bath (see page 28). This will remove any stress and emotional or mental remnants that you might have picked up from the environment. Apply the "cutting the cord" technique to detach from past events or objects (see page 51). Take a walk in nature, breathe, and smile.

take action now

If you have not begun the clearing process, start small by following these suggestions:

1. Take a slow walk around your space. Identify the kinds of clutter you have. Is it physical, symbolic, or energy clutter? In which rooms do you find the most clutter? Why are you keeping it? Do you have storage units within each room?

2. Give your home or office a good spring-cleaning. Make everything shine like new.

3. Clear some simple clutter: take out the trash, throw away junk mail and expired coupons, discard prescriptions more than a year old, and put dry cleaning in your car.

4. Ask a friend to help you clear your clutter and offer to do something for him or for her in return. Treat your friend to dinner and a movie after the session or go dancing.

5. Donate old books to the library, clothes to charity, and old computers to a school in need. Let go and create good karma at the same time. Don't forget, the donations are tax deductions, too.

6. Make a list of the people you need to speak to, a list of errands you need to run, a list of appointments you need to make, and follow through. Do what needs to be done and then cross the item off your list.

four:

energy solutions and enhancements

One of the main goals in feng shui is to maximize the strengths and minimize the weaknesses in your space. Every environment has both positive and negative elements that affect your daily life. The great news is that ninety-five percent of the weaknesses are fixable. In this chapter, you will learn proven energy solutions and enhancements that restore balance and power to your environment.

Some people avoid learning about feng shui because they fear change. They worry their home will require major renovations they cannot afford. Perhaps they will be instructed to paint the entire living room red or relinquish something they love such as a fantastic view or high ceilings. These are merely fears, not truths. Often a well-placed plant, water fountain, or lamp can shift the energy in a room. You are aware of how your life is unfolding. By discovering how your environment may be influencing you, you have the power to make changes if necessary. Knowledge is power.

Every space is unique in structure and energy. Therefore, a solution that generates amazing results for you may produce slightly different ones for your neighbor. Experiment. If you have a choice between two or three enhancements, pick one and stick with it for a month or two. If you feel better, keep it in place; if not, try another one. Explore all of the possibilities. Use your intuition to decide what works best for you at each phase of your life. Feng shui promotes balance, beauty, and healthy energy

 ## unsuitable energy

Feng shui teaches you to recognize energy patterns in your space. You begin to discover how energy feels and moves. Is it moving fast or is it slow? Is it heavy or light? Is it depleted or flourishing? You will set out on an expedition to understand how the energy in your surroundings may be affecting the way you think, feel, and act. Ultimately, you may discover energy reasons for the way your life is proceeding.

The following types of energy need to be altered, moderated, balanced, or stimulated to create harmony and balance in your environment. As you go from room to room, you will come across situations where these types of energies exist.

Sharp energy—created by pointed objects or sharp corners on walls and furniture

Fast-moving energy—created by long hallways or staircases

Oppressive energy—created by exposed beams and low ceilings

Stagnant energy—created by clutter and excessive furniture

Missing energy—created by deficient energy centers or corners

Since these energies may have physical, emotional, or financial implications for you and your family, you must learn how to counteract them. This chapter introduces you to the tools you will use to apply feng shui to your space. It helps you understand why you should hang a crystal under an exposed beam or a plant in a stagnant corner. It lays the groundwork for implementing enhancements throughout the rest of the book.

The laws of energy are always working. They may or may not be beneficial to you. Feng shui offers guidelines for correcting energy patterns that are unfavorable. You have the choice to follow all or some of them, depending on how they make you feel. You will be able to determine how to speed up, slow down, soften, and balance energy in your space. Certain solutions will be easy to incorporate; others might not be so easy. Some may look fantastic; others may be a bit bizarre. One of my teachers admits, "Feng shui isn't always going to be convenient." The goal is to see and feel results.

solutions and enhancements for equilibrium

Achieving equilibrium in your environment is an important aspect of feng shui. The solutions and enhancements in the coming pages have been used to correct the flow of energy for thousands of years. Included are the ones I believe are the strongest and most effective.

Multitaskers—mirrors, crystals, and wind chimes
Energizers—plants, light, and water features
Stabilizers—heavy or solid objects
Illuminators—color, symbolic objects, and artwork

When placed properly, these enhancements will actively direct the energy to support you in manifesting your dreams and goals. You must believe that the enhancement will do its job. Work to strengthen this belief. Allow the possibility of transformation to permeate your thoughts and emotions.

In this chapter, you will learn the general characteristics of each enhancement. Specific placement, instructions, and explanations will be presented in depth as you move through each subsequent chapter of the book.

multitaskers

Multitaskers, as I refer to them, are extremely helpful in feng shui. Sometimes people refer to mirrors as the "aspirin" of feng shui. They fix a variety of energy problems. Crystals and wind chimes spread energy evenly throughout any space. By learning how and when to use all three of these enhancements, you will be well on your way to creating space that circulates positive energy.

Multitaskers expand, circulate, multiply, attract, reflect, and diffuse energy. Depending on the specific energy pattern, its location within the space, and the way it relates to other objects, each multitasker will influence energy in a variety of ways. Feng shui is not all black and white. A gray area exists because of the unique characteristics within each environment. By learning the tendency of each enhancement, you will be able to balance your space more effectively.

Mirrors

Mirrors serve many purposes in feng shui. They influence energy by:

    Activating

    Circulating

    Reflecting

    Deflecting

    Amplifying

    Multiplying

    Doubling

    Projecting

Mirrors bring light into a dark space, push away negative energy, activate a stagnant room, energize a missing corner, and double positive and negative energies. It's important to be cognizant of what kinds of energy you are symbolically doubling or multiplying. For instance, if you place a mirror behind a plant, you are doubling living energy. However, if a mirror reflects garbage, you are doubling the trash. This is not recommended.

general tips for mirrors:

- Hang a mirror large enough to reflect your entire body with ample room above your head.
- Place a mirror to reflect a beautiful view of nature, plants, and flowers.

RIGHT: This large mirror over the fireplace activates positive energy by lifting your gaze, bringing in natural light, reflecting artwork on the opposite wall, and doubling the vitality and beauty of the flowers in the room.

- Keep all mirrors sparkling clean, so you see yourself clearly.
- Hang a mirror in a small room to expand the space.
- Use a frame or fabric to cover or drape any sharp edges of a mirror.
- Avoid mirrored tiles; they break your reflection into pieces.
- Remove cracked, broken, or warped mirrors; they distort your image.
- Do not allow clutter to accumulate in front of a mirror; it doubles it.

Feng shui makes use of two additional types of reflectors. Convex mirrors are slightly rounded, so they disperse energy in many directions. Because they are wide-angled, they are used to divert negative energy away from a specific area. For example, if you have difficult neighbors living above you, and you want to separate yourself from them, place a convex mirror in a plant facing upward to stop their energy from pouring down. Convex mirrors are used inside and outside the home. You can purchase them at drugstores and auto supply stores.

The other type of reflector is a gazing ball, which looks like a silver globe. The round, mirrored surface deflects large amounts of undesired energy away from the outside of the home. You might use a gazing ball if your home sits at the end of a cul-de-sac. To divert the fast-moving energy streaming towards your home, set a gazing ball next to your front door. Gazing balls, along with a stand, can be purchased at garden centers and nurseries. The stand supports the ball, raising it to an appropriate height.

RIGHT: A round-faceted crystal hung in a window circulates energy throughout the room while creating brilliant rainbows each time it catches the sun.

BELOW: To deflect large amounts of negative energy streaming into your home, place a stand with gazing ball in front of your door. Gazing balls are best used if your home sits at the end of a cul-de-sac, T-junction, or dead-end street.

Crystals

Feng shui crystals are round, faceted, clear glass crystals that refract light and circulate energy. Crystals are usually hung from ceilings at specific lengths to influence energy by:

Attracting

Activating

Holding

Dispersing

Circulating

Crystals slow down energy in staircases, disperse fast-moving energy in long hallways, stimulate stagnant corners, circulate energy within a room, soften sharp edges, and create rainbows of color when hung in windows.

general tips for crystals

- Use a spherical shape as opposed to a teardrop one to disperse energy in a balanced way.
- Don't use asymmetrical crystals; they can cause an imbalance.
- Hang crystals from windows and ceilings with clear fishing wire to draw less attention.
- Use crystal chandeliers as alternatives to crystals.
- Clean crystals twice a month with salt water or rubbing alcohol.

The common feng shui sizes are 0.8 inch (20mm) and 1-round inch (30mm). Use a bigger crystal to moderate a larger area. Crystals send waves of energy in equal currents in all directions. You can purchase them in spiritual bookstores or on the Internet.

Wind Chimes

Wind chimes are important conductors in feng shui. They affect energy by:

Moderating

Dispersing

Attracting

feng shui your pet

Dogs, cats, birds, rabbits, and other pets offer unconditional love, companionship, protection, and positive energy to the home. Their movement and individual sounds, barks, meows, and chirps help to circulate energy to every corner. For good feng shui, your pet should be clean, smell good, and have its own place within the environment. Create a space for your pet with a bed, mat, rug, or cage. Do not allow your animal's toys to take over the house. If you own a cat, make sure the litter is hooded and kept fresh. Having a dog is a great way to stay in shape because you'll take daily walks. However, make sure your dog is well behaved. It would not be advantageous for your dog to scare away potential love or work interests! Many times, the dog becomes a reflection of the owner. What is your pet saying about you?

Metal wind chimes made of long, hollow, cylindrical tubes are best. They slow down and disperse energy, deflect negative energy away from the outside the house, and circulate energy in closets and basements. When hung at the door, they send out a positive message. Chimes summon prosperity when hung above the stove. Clay, wooden, and porcelain chimes do not have the same effect.

Wind chimes come in an assortment of shapes and sizes with varying sounds, tones, and pitch. When choosing one for outside of the home, make sure it is pleasing and harmonious to you. You don't need to hear the sound when it is hung indoors. The metal of the tubes is used to circulate the energy. You can purchase wind chimes at garden centers, drugstores, and specialty gift shops.

sounds of delight

Sound vibration is very powerful. As sounds pass through your personal energy field, they can relax or stimulate you. They enhance your mood in many ways. You may play music for inspiration, to unwind, to create romance, or to facilitate learning. Soft music soothes your soul as you lie in the bath; a strong drumbeat invigorates your body as you wash your car. In the same way, pleasing sounds calm or energize your environment. These feng shui enhancements consist of wind chimes, bells, music, water fountains, nature sounds, and your own beautiful singing voice! Just the sound of birds chirping outside the window can uplift your mood. Additionally, you can play a CD with the sound of OM after an argument or clutter clearing session to "clear the air" and disintegrate negative energy. Discover the sounds or songs that enliven your spirit and play them regularly.

energizers

From a feng shui standpoint, the three best energizers for any environment are plants, light, and moving water. Feng shui is based on the idea of giving and receiving. As you give positive energy to your surroundings, your intention is to receive energy in the form of health, wealth, success, and love. Since energy moves in a circular motion throughout each room, it misses the corners, and thus they become stagnant. Placing plants, lamps, and water features in the corners immediately uplifts the energy and guides it into the circular rotation. This elevates the energy in the whole environment.

These energizers will stimulate, enhance, uplift and produce energy in your surroundings. If I could give only one piece of feng shui advice, I would recommend bringing as many energizers into your space as you can. You will immediately feel a sense of ease, balance, and harmony.

Plants and Flowers

Life force within nature uplifts and harmonizes the environment. Plants give oxygen and recycle air, evoke serenity, and circulate healing energy. The more plants you have, the better. They affect energy by:

RIGHT: To uplift and harmonize energy in any room, place thriving plants with rounded leaves in the corners. Position plants on a table or bookshelf for optimum benefit and circulation.

pointers for plants

You will discover that plants are a great cure-all in feng shui. The rule to remember is that wherever you need more energy, add a plant. The best types are upward-growing plants with round leaves. You don't want plants that have droopy leaves. The worst types are stiff and spiky plants. Do not use cacti. On the other hand, pothos is one of the best and hardiest plants to own. Throw out all dead plants, dried flowers, and potpourri. They are dead energy. You may use live or silk plants to soften the sharp corners of furniture. Here are a few spots where adding plants will increase the flow:

- **Corners**—Place a plant in a corner to avoid stagnation and to increase and lift the energy.
- **Bathrooms**—Hang a plant in the bathroom to increase healthy energy.
- **Long hallway**—Stagger large bushy plants in a hallway to slow down energy.
- **Sharp protruding corner**—Place a plant beside a pointed corner to soften the energy.
- **Desks**—Add a plant next to your computer for rejuvenation and oxygen.

Fresh flowers add vibrancy, color, and life to your surroundings. Silk flowers and plants are good feng shui. They provide beauty, color, and circulate positive energy without weekly care. By placing silk and live foliage together in your space, you have less to water. Silk flowers and plants can be just as beautiful as live ones. Combine them creatively, and your friends will never know the difference. At the end of this chapter, you will find a list of some of the best feng shui houseplants as well as some you want to avoid.

Uplifting
Harmonizing
Increasing
Stimulating
Circulating
Dispersing

In feng shui, healthy plants and flowers bring in new opportunities. With specific placement, plants enhance health, love, success, and wealth. Plants neutralize the harmful effects of electromagnetic fields coming from appliances and electronics. They raise energy in stagnant corners and slow energy down in long corridors and stairwells. Thriving plants add warmth and charm to your home or office.

energy solutions and enhancements

flowers for your spirit

Experiment using the color palette in chapter one to pick the right flowers to enhance your mood. For instance, try pink roses for love, red gladiolas for motivation, yellow daisies and sunflowers for happiness, blue hydrangeas for relaxation, purple orchids for spirituality, orange marigolds for inspiration, and white calla lilies for purification. Gardenia, tuberose, and freesia offer blissful scents. Give yourself the gift of weekly flowers to bring exuberant energy and color into your home or office.

Silk Solutions

Silk does a great job of keeping one type of energy away from another. For instance, you want to keep the "waste" energy in the bathroom to a minimum. Placing small silk plants on both sides of the base of the toilet insulates the energy. Keeping it close to the floor will help prevent it from contaminating healthy energy. In addition, silk fabric or vines wrapped around the banister of a staircase will slow down the energy. When hung below exposed beams, silk fabric can protect you by keeping the oppressive energy from bearing down on you. While silk plants and flowers circulate energy, they do not produce it.

Lighting and Lamps

Light, especially sunlight, lifts the energy of the room, brightens your spirit, expands the space, and inspires new ideas. Light affects energy by:

Uplifting

Stimulating

Activating

Producing

Increasing

Within an environment, light is produced by incandescent and halogen bulbs, candles, fireplaces, lamps, and natural sunlight. Light raises oppressive energy from low ceilings, uplifts energy in a dark space, activates a stagnant corner, attracts attention outside the front door, and produces energy in a missing corner. Night-lights kept on twenty-four hours a day energize small spaces without using too much electricity. They are especially useful in bathrooms, closets, basements, attics, and hall-

LEFT: Vibrant red tulips invigorate this otherwise muted dining room.

ways. Additionally, fireplaces and candles generate energy from the light and heat that they produce. Adding scented candles to various places in your home will boost the energy and provide relaxation at the same time.

Since most people spend ninety percent of their life indoors, it is essential to get proper exposure to healthy light. The best light is natural sunlight. Open drapes and windows and add skylights for extra exposure. Full-spectrum light bulbs are the healthiest type of light because they simulate sunlight. They are highly recommended to energize your space, body, and mood. Use full-spectrum bulbs in the areas where you spend the majority of your time. They can be purchased at specialty lighting stores and natural food stores. Another beneficial light comes from tungsten-halogen lamps. They project a bright white light that is similar to daylight and good for general illumination. Avoid using florescent lighting whenever possible. The pulsing ultraviolet and blue rays cause eyestrain, headaches, and fatigue.

Water Features

Water, aligned with prosperity and health, is a key element in feng shui. Water fountains and aquariums are very powerful energizers when placed properly. Bubbling water affects energy by:

Producing

Stimulating

Activating

Harmonizing

Incorporating water features inside and outside your environment brings beauty to your eyes, music to your ears, and harmony to your spirit. Moving water can provide energy to a static corner, stimulate your finances, and replenish energy that is missing from an area of your home. Since water symbolizes money, the bubbling water in fountains and aquariums creates a continuous circulation of wealth and abundance around you.

A water fountain in your living space invites nature indoors. The sound of water gently splashing against pebbles masks unwanted noise and increases negative ions, creating a sense of well-being and ease. Keep the water clean and running continuously. A few drops of bleach in the water

LEFT: A radiant combination of sunlight, lamps, and fire strengthens the energy in your home, evoking a more positive emotional outlook for you and your family.

helps to keep it sparkling clean. You want to make sure your "finances" aren't murky or stagnant. Aquariums are considered a double enhancement since they combine bubbling water with the life force of colorful swimming fish. Fish symbolize wealth and are considered good luck. Now you understand why you see aquariums in most Asian restaurants. In addition, water fountains and fish ponds placed outside the home can increase prosperity and abundance.

stabilizers

Many times in life you wish you could have something that would settle the waters, so to speak. When certain predicaments arise, instead of becoming frantic, you need to slow down and proceed with your feet firmly on the ground. In

ABOVE: Indoors or out, a pleasing water fountain can soothe your nerves, increase your finances, and stimulate forward momentum in your life.

BELOW: Large, heavy pottery positioned at the bottom of a stairwell will slow down and stabilize speeding energy that may be heading out the door.

the same way, when the energy in your home is unstable, it can seep into the rest of your life. Placing heavy, solid objects in various areas can steady a tumultuous relationship, health problem, or job issue.

Sometimes, the energy in your home is actually moving too quickly. This can cause an imbalance. You may feel overwhelmed or irritated in a particular room. Place stabilizers outside to slow down and calm the energy rushing towards your front door. Heavy objects absorb and block forceful energy, allowing you to feel solid and in control of your daily life.

Heavy and Solid Objects

Weighty objects, placed correctly within your house affect fast-moving energy by:

Slowing down

Calming

Grounding

Securing

Stabilizing

Energy often becomes erratic and needs taming. Heavy objects placed in long corridors and at the bottom of staircases stabilize the space. In rooms above a carport, they can be set in each corner to ground energy coming from the constant movement of cars underneath. Solid objects also encourage a project to materialize.

Types of heavy objects to use include stone, large pottery, rocks, big pieces of furniture, planters, columns, wooden trunks, pianos, and glass, iron, and stone sculptures and statues. Natural stones and rocks have additional value since they hold the natural energy of the earth. Pottery, stone sculptures, and large rocks can be purchased at garden and lumber centers.

On the other hand, too many weighty objects can cause a heavy feeling in the home and may bring

things to a standstill. Walk around your space and notice where you have large pieces of furniture such as an entertainment center, bookshelf, armoire, or dresser. The energy may be stuck in these places. Simply adding a plant to the top of a large piece of furniture will move the energy. Once again, balance is necessary.

illuminators

To illuminate is to enlighten, vitalize, and inspire. In feng shui, color, symbolic objects, and artwork are considered illuminators. These enhancements make all the difference in the energy that your home exudes. Imagine your home is a blank canvas ready for your creative hand. You can use color, symbolic objects, and artwork to paint the life you want to live. Never underestimate the power that they have on your subconscious mind. Everything you see creates a certain psychological and emotional effect, many times beyond your level of awareness.

Illuminators can motivate, rejuvenate, and harmonize you and your space. They can instigate either joy or unhappiness. For example, a dark, gray kitchen affects you differently than a sunny, yellow one. A picture of a growling tiger evokes a different emotion than a litter of kittens. Now is the time to evaluate your surroundings and how they affect you. Observe the colors, objects, and art in your home to identify their impact upon you. If they do not encourage your well-being and forward momentum, you may want to reconsider keeping them. Make a conscious choice to create a healthy environment that supports you in all your endeavors.

Color

Color is a significant element in feng shui. It influences you and the energy of your space by:

Uplifting

Relaxing

Motivating

Inspiring

Feng shui promotes the use of color in specific ways. In chapter one, you discovered how color affects you psychologically and influences your emotions. Likewise, the colors used in your surroundings can make a major difference in the energy in the home. In the chapters five and six, you will

ABOVE: A red living room activates energy and stimulates your pulse, promoting lively conversation, social interaction, and family activity.

learn about the nine energy centers and their corresponding colors. As a preview, bold red enhances the wealth and fame centers; deep blue strengthens knowledge; solid black supports career; soft pink stimulates love; and refreshing green promotes health and family.

Certain colors are recommended for certain types of rooms. As you travel from room to room in each chapter, you will discover the colors that are most favorable. For instance, green is easy on the eyes because it surrounds us in nature. It is wonderful for rooms in which you spend a great deal of time such as the dining room and the living room. Because blue is calming and peaceful, it is appropriate for the bedroom. Blue in the kitchen helps to subdue your appetite. In contrast, a vibrant splash of red at the front door encourages visitors to drop in. Red is an active color that pops out and says, "My home is lively."

Before you make a commitment to paint your walls a specific color, test the color on a small piece of wood and walk around the room with it. Live with it for a while to see how it affects you. Colors will look different in natural as opposed to artificial light, so experiment with them during the day and at night.

Over and above the feng shui recommendations, allow your heart to assist you in choosing colors you love. Enhance your walls with color or spread it across your home with rugs, pillows, furniture, art, candles, pottery, dishes, bedding, and drapery.

Symbolic Objects

Symbolic objects are items that affect you physically, emotionally, mentally, or spiritually. Feng shui teaches you to use artwork, photos,

ABOVE: Soft blue perfectly suits the bedroom. The cool shade is associated with serenity, calm, and introspection, allowing for a restful night's sleep.

TOP RIGHT: An elegant family heirloom such as a Queen Elizabeth tea set may both elicit fond memories and afford you a feeling of wealth and grandeur.

BOTTOM RIGHT: A statue of the Three Graces symbolizes joy, grace, beauty, and charm.

mementos, and decorative objects to symbolize what you want to manifest. As your intentions become clear, write down your goals and think about what symbols you can use to represent them. For instance, if you want a romantic relationship, your symbolism might be a photo of two people in love, a book of poetry, or a painting of an island in the Pacific. If your goal is to buy a new house, your symbols might include real estate magazines, pictures of your ideal home. When you place these items in your environment, you are actively and purposefully programming your entire being to achieve your goals.

Remember that any object you love or any object that is beautiful to you becomes an enhancement that can inspire you. What represents love to one person may be totally different to another. This book contains many feng shui suggestions. Feel free to combine them with your own personal preferences and innate creativity to produce solutions that work for you.

Artwork

Art is a powerful tool to relax, motivate, and inspire you. According to the principles of feng shui, the artwork that you display should be positive, colorful, and abundant. Avoid artwork that depicts poverty, death, depression, lonely images, or bleak scenes. Seascapes and landscapes bring in nature and soothe the soul. The expansiveness of these scenes opens up the space and elicits a feeling of freedom as you "look out the window." Colorful gardens with a multitude of flowers and trees are excellent feng shui.

The two most meaningful areas to display art are across from your front entrance and opposite your bed. Every time you enter and leave your home, you should be greeted by your favorite piece of art. In your bedroom, you will be inspired as you fall asleep and when you awaken. Surround yourself with artwork that makes you happy.

pothos   peace lily   dieffenbachia   ficus

good house plants

good—low light required

Chinese Evergreen—*Aglaonema Modestum elegans*
Dumb Cane—*Dieffenbachia amoena*
Hi Color Dieffenbachia—*Dieffenbachia amoena* (Hi color)
Tropic Snow Dieffenbachia—*Dieffenbachia amoena*
  (Tropic Snow)
Camille Dieffenbachia—*Dieffenbachia maculata Camille*
Impact Exotica Dieffenbachia—*Dieffenbachia maculata*
  Exotica Compacta
Green Pothos—*Epipremnun aureum* "Jade"
Marble Queen Pothos—*Epipremnun aureum*
  "Marble Queen"
Golden Pothos—*Epipremnun aureum Scindapsus Aureus*
Rubber Plant—*Ficus elastica* "Decora"
Peace Lily—*Spathiphyllum* sp.
Nephthytis—*Syngonium podophyllum*
Corn Plant—*Dracaena fragrans massangeana*
Lucky Bamboo

good—medium light required

Amate Schefflera—*Brassaia actinophylla* "amate"
Jade Plant—*Crassula argentea*
Norma Croton—*Codiaeum variegatum* "norma"
Fiddle Leaf Fig—*Ficus lyrata*
Wandering Jew—*Zebrina pendula*

Pink Splash Polka Dot Plant—*Hypoestes phyllostachya*
  "pink splash"
Red Emerald Philodendron—*Philodendron* "Red Emerald"
Heartleaf Philodendron—*Philodendron scandens*
  oxycardium
Money Plant—*Philodendron scanden*
Dallas Fern—*Nephrolepis exaltata* "Dallas Jewel"

good—high light required

Bamboo Palms—*Chamaedorea erumpens*
Weeping Fig—*Ficus benjamina*
Zebra Plant—*Aphelandra squarrosa*
Prayer Plants—*Maranta leuconeura* var. erythroneura
Mums—*Chrysanthemum* sp.
Pointsettia—*Euphorbia pulcherrima*
African Violet—*Saintpaulia ionantha*
Anthurium—*Anthurium* sp.
Begonias—*Begonia* sp.
Orchids—*Orchidaceae*

cactus   fan palm   venus fly trap   snake plant

house plants to avoid

All Cacti—*Cactaceae*
Venus Flytrap—*Dionaea muscipula*
Dragon Tree—*Dracaena marginata*
Snake Plants/Common Sansevieria—*Sanservieria trifasciata*
European Fan Palm—*Chamaeropsis humilis*
Bromeliads—*Bromeliaceae*

the bagua

Feng shui is based on the premise that your space mirrors your life. As you know, the objects and energy in your environment impact your life's progress. Some of you want to stimulate your health and wealth; others wish to invigorate their love life, spiritual connection, or career. Now is the time to begin putting enhancements to work for you.

The bagua, from the *I Ching* (*The Chinese Book of Changes*), is a feng shui tool that helps manifest your dreams and goals. The bagua provides a blueprint and a formula to enhance nine significant areas in your life. Each area has a corresponding energy center within your home environment.

The bagua is essentially a map that you superimpose on the layout of a house, apartment, guest home, office, or room. It indicates the location of nine energy centers. Once you find the energy centers, you can enliven them by adding specific feng shui enhancements. Think of the bagua as a board game for life. The board is divided into nine areas. At the outset, you decide which areas you want to focus on. When you use the correct colors, symbols, and energizers in your chosen areas, you win the jackpot. The object of the game is to have the right feng shui combination. Translate the idea of this game into your life and expect miracles.

PREVIOUS PAGE: Plants, colorful pillows, and a statue of a Buddha create an energy center that concentrates on spiritual knowledge.

RIGHT: The bagua is a map consisting of nine energy centers. These centers correspond to specific areas of life that you can strengthen with feng shui enhancements.

the nine centers of the bagua

Health and Well-Being (center)
Love and Relationships (rear right)
Career (front middle)
Wealth and Prosperity (rear left)
Family (middle left)
Creativity and Children (middle right)
Knowledge and Wisdom (front left)
Fame and Reputation (rear middle)
Helpful People (front right)

By removing obstacles, circulating positive energy, and programming your dreams and goals into each area, you are creating excellent feng shui. Your creativity, excitement, and belief in the enhancements will help you to manifest your dreams and goals in a more powerful way.

During this process of applying the principles of feng shui to your space, you need to blend the masculine and feminine energies within you. Balance your driving desire to achieve your goals with a sense of peace and harmony. The masculine energy resembles a straight line heading for a specific destination. It takes constant action and aims at a target. On the

wealth and prosperity

fame and reputation

love and relationships

family

health and well-being

creativity and children

knowledge and wisdom

career

helpful people

other hand, the feminine energy is circular and flowing. It is receptive, playful, and enjoys the present moment. Feng shui connects both principles. While fulfilling your wishes, remember to simply bask in the beauty and vibrant energy surrounding you.

 ## energy center locations

Finding your energy centers begins with drawing a simple overhead sketch of your home to identify the shape. You must include all attached spaces, including the garage, room additions, and screened-in porches. Every area that has a roof and sides and is attached to the main structure should be included. When you have drawn the basic shape of your living space, divide it into nine equal parts.

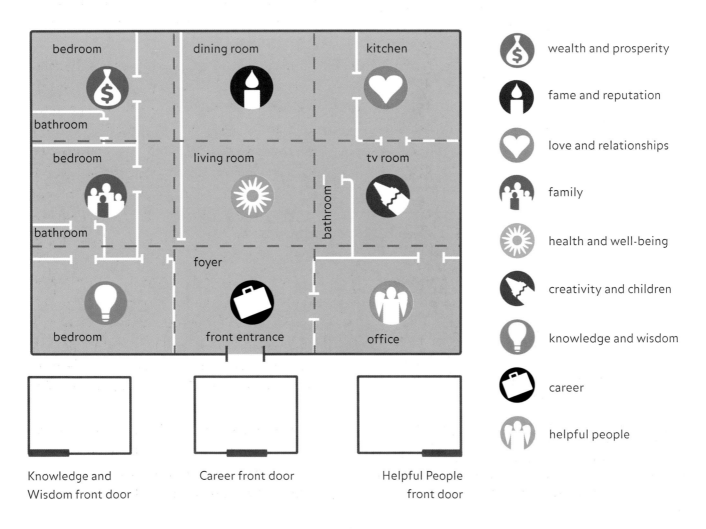

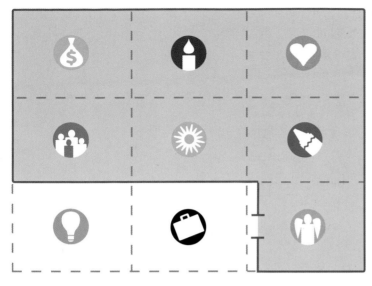

Helpful People front door

ABOVE: If your front door opens into a vestibule in which you must turn in order to enter the main body of your home, rotate the bagua map to fit over the main structure of the home. In the instance shown here, you will enter into the Helpful People center, but Career and Knowledge centers are missing from the structure.

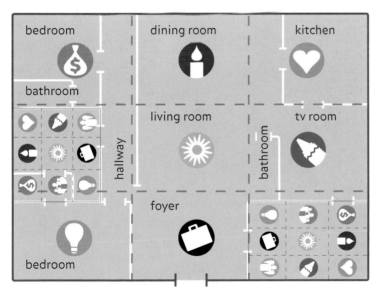

Career front door

ABOVE: When you apply the bagua to specific rooms, make sure you orient it from the door to that room. The bagua overlaid on the left-hand middle room and the bagua overlaid on the right-hand bottom room are placed differently due to the door locations for those specific rooms.

In order to locate the energy centers, you must determine how to place the bagua over the layout of your home. Your front door determines the proper placement. Although you may use an alternate door to enter your home, you should use the formal front door as a starting point to determine the layout of the bagua. Lay the bagua on top of the drawing of your house so that the front door is in Knowledge and Wisdom, Career, or Helpful People. These three centers will always be on the bottom of your drawing. Once you figure out which center your front door opens into, it is easy to locate the rest. If your home is large, one center may include two or three rooms. If you have a smaller house or apartment, you may discover three centers show up in one room.

The main or first floor of the home is the most important level for the bagua because the first floor retains the most energy. The constant influx of energy through the front door is one of the factors along with the amount of activity that occurs there. In addition to applying the bagua to the entire main level, it can also be superimposed on specific rooms. For example, if your house has more than one story, you can use the bagua for each room on subsequent levels. In each instance, orient the bagua from the main door to that particular room. If the room has more than one entrance, choose the one that is used most frequently. In most cases, the bagua to each room will be different than how it is placed on the main level. They don't need to match (see below left).

When you stand in the doorway looking into any space, point to the back left corner to find Wealth and Prosperity and point to the back right corner to find Love and Relationships.

missing energy centers

In order for each area of your life to advance, you must properly energize every center in the bagua. If your home is in the shape of a square or a rectangle, you will notice that all centers are located within the structure. This is ideal. You need to keep this in mind when building a house or remodeling. Some of you may have discovered that your home is not a perfectly equal shape. Because many homes and apartments are irregularly shaped, some of the centers are missing. This can create challenges or deficiencies in the corresponding area of your life, but don't fret. With feng shui enhancements, you can find many ways to correct the situation and reverse the prognosis.

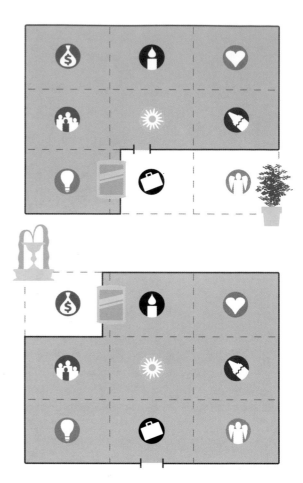

When areas of the bagua fall outside the structure, you must symbolically and literally fill in the empty space and "square off" the home. You'll need to use stabilizers and energizers to bring the center back into your life. These enhancers will allow you to ground the missing center and to provide it with energy for that particular area of your life. If you have the ability to add items to the outside of your home, you can anchor the missing center with a physical landmark. This can be a lamppost, tree, large potted plant, sculpture, water fountain, boulder, gazebo, or garden wall. Place the enhancement exactly where the two walls of your home would meet if they extended out to make a perfect square (see right).

In apartments, where you cannot reconcile the missing center outdoors, you can symbolically fix it by placing a large mirror on the wall closest to the missing center. A mirror opens up the space to encompass the part that is missing. Place a plant in front of the mirror to increase the energy. You can use this solution for any room that has a missing corner (see right).

bagua layers

Layering is a term used when you apply the bagua in multiple rooms to increase a specific area of your life. It is akin to backing up files on your computer to protect them or to applying three coats of paint to secure the color. For example, if you want to stimulate your career and finances, you'll want to energize those centers on the main level as well as in individual rooms for added support. In addition, you must layer when you are missing

$ wealth and prosperity

fame and reputation

love and relationships

family

health and well-being

creativity and children

knowledge and wisdom

career

helpful people

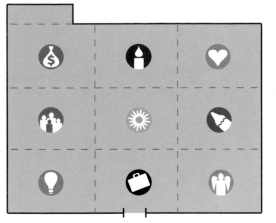
Career front door

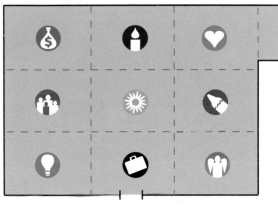
Career front door

a center. Imagine that you are missing the Love and Relationships center on the main level. You'll need to energize the Love Center in other rooms, including the living room and bedroom.

fortunate extensions

You may be lucky and discover that your house has an addition as opposed to a missing space. An extra area protruding from your home is considered favorable. The center that is closest to the extension gains a significant increase in energy. However, sometimes it is difficult to determine if an area is missing or the one beside it is protruding. The rule of thumb is that when the protruding area is equal to one third or less of the corresponding side of the house, it is considered an extension. In other words, if the protruding area is more than one third of the corresponding side of the home, the area next to it becomes a missing center. Having an extension in Wealth, Love, or Career is very advantageous (see left).

corresponding rooms and energy centers

As you match each room with a center, notice if there is a link between how it looks in comparison with that specific area of your life. Is the room overused or underused? Is it full of clutter? Is it neglected? How is it decorated? Do you love that room or do you dislike it? Do you notice positive or negative symbolism? As you discover where each center is located, determine if there is a correlation between the center and how that area is maintained. For instance, if your kitty litter resides in the Love and Relationships center, what does that indicate about your love life? Similarly, if your Wealth and Prosperity center is full of dirty laundry, how could that affect your current money situation? Begin to contemplate which items you may want to remove or to add now that you understand the symbolism.

bathrooms

The phrase "don't flush your money down the toilet" is taken seriously in feng shui. Water, which represents prosperity, is abundant in the bathroom. If the door to the bathroom remains open, energy from the rest of your home flows into the room and into the running water. This may seem profitable. However, the water escapes down the sink, shower, and tub drains, taking your money with it. The toilet is the most harmful element to your finances because the opening is large and the water suction is powerful. Keeping the toilet seat down and the door closed are crucial to boosting your wealth. Your goal is to divert the positive energy away from the bathroom and the toilet.

When an energy center is located in a bathroom, you may experience a drain in that area of your life. For instance, if your Wealth center is in the toilet, you may encounter challenges with your finances or have trouble holding on to money. You may be spending money faster than you can earn it. Simply stated, it is draining out of your life and bank account. Pay attention to bathrooms located in Wealth, Love, Career, Fame, and Health. If a bathroom is in your Love and Relationships center, you may have trouble establishing or maintaining a relationship. If it is located in Career, you may have difficulty closing deals; in Fame, your reputation could be tarnished. Most importantly, if you have a bathroom in the center of your home, your health could be negatively affected. Do not dismay. There are many solutions to counteract these obstacles so the bathrooms will work in your favor. Closing them off from the rest of the home and energizing them is the key to abundance and prosperity.

power bathrooms

The following recommendations serve as a foundation for energizing all bathrooms. You will be inspired to add specific enhancements depending on their location and your personal style as you go through the book.

- Keep the bathroom door closed and toilet seat down at all times.
- Keep a small lamp or night-light on twenty-four hours a day.
- Place a healthy plant higher than the toilet, but not on top of the toilet.
- Hang a round, faceted crystal above the sink, shower, and tub drains five inches from the ceiling.
- Place a small silk plant, flowers, or fabric on both sides of the toilet base to insulate toilet energy.
- Place mirrors in the bathroom to activate and circulate energy.
- Add specific enhancements for each center.

a fresh start

Your thoughts and beliefs create your reality. What you choose to focus on determines your quality of life. I believe that the best results are achieved when your thoughts stay upbeat and confident. Even if you must use what seems like Herculean will power, I feel it is vital to choose right now to disengage from negative beliefs, thought patterns, and cynicism so that feng shui can take hold and improve your life. It is not that easy to just let them go. Make a conscious effort to use feng shui to change your thought patterns. Rearrange your thinking to allow the good to come in.

Breathe possibility and excitement into every enhancement and expect it to work. Here are a few suggestions to help you:
- Say, "Yes," three times with every change you make.
- Say, "Thank you," as if your desire has already manifested.
- Affirm a positive outcome every time you walk past your enhancement.

Your ability to create a loving relationship, succeed in your career, increase your income, nurture a devoted family, and become spiritually fulfilled is at your doorstep.

environmental anchors

Environmental anchors are special, meaningful objects you place in your home or office that affirm and promote positive thoughts, feelings, and images. You will program your specific intention into these objects and use them as symbols for your own goals and dreams. Placed in the correct spot according to the bagua, you are actively transforming your home, state of mind, and entire life.

Any object can serve as an environmental anchor for you. You must infuse it with your own meaning so it sends a positive message back to you on a daily basis. Here are a few examples of environmental anchors:
- A college diploma in your Career center evokes a mental picture of securing the right job.
- A heart-shaped vase with fresh flowers in your Love and Relationships center infuses you with romance.
- A bubbling water fountain in your Wealth and Prosperity center summons images of your money increasing in the stock market.
- A picture of angels in the Helpful People center reminds you that you are guided at every moment.

Be open and ready for these environmental anchors to translate into wealth, health, and happiness in your life.

take action now

1. **Sketch an overhead** layout of your home and divide it into nine equal parts.

2. **Superimpose the bagua** from the position of the front door to find out if you have any missing centers or fortunate extensions.

3. **Decide which centers you want** to layer for maximum results.

4. **Locate your bathrooms** to see where they fall in the bagua. To increase your prosperity, close the bathroom doors and put the toilet seats down.

5. **Walk around your house** to find environmental anchors to employ right away. A special object with positive symbolism will do the trick.

the nine energy centers

Think of the bagua as your manifestation machine, a vehicle to materialize your goals. In chapter two, you discovered the areas of your life that you want to enhance for your happiness and fulfillment. Now is the time to apply your intentions to energize the centers of the bagua. You are purposefully deciding what you want and how your home can support you in attaining it. You'll find it helpful to remember that what goes around, comes around. In other words, you must offer that which you desire to others.

Contribute a portion of it into the world, and it will return to you. If you want respect, extend it to others. If you desire love, express it. If you covet money, share it. Giving is a surefire way to continue receiving blessings. Keep the giving principle alive during the entire feng shui process.

Again, make it a habit to clear clutter and garbage before you energize. As you provide energy and positive symbolism for each center, you are programming your home, subconscious mind, and the universe to make your desires a reality.

PREVIOUS PAGE: A plant with leaves that shoot upward introduces living energy and vivid color to any of the bagua's centers.

manifestation techniques

Creativity and imagination are key ingredients in the recipe for extraordinary feng shui. You should implement inspiring techniques to fortify the energy in each center of the bagua. To reinforce the enhancements, the following tools are helpful. Here is a brief explanation of how and why they work.

intentional writing

Words have great power. You make your goals and desires more concrete with the written word, and they manifest more rapidly. These affirmative statements must be hand-written with a red pen and deposited in a red envelope for activation. Place the envelope next to or underneath a plant to multiply its strength. General examples will be offered for each center but you can personalize them to fit your own goals and dreams. Be specific and cultivate an attitude of gratitude in your writing.

manifestation board

This is a corkboard with a collection of beautiful and inspi-rational pictures from magazines, sayings, quotes, pictures

of famous people, postcards, and drawings depicting your desires for a specific area of your life. Displaying your wishes and goals in one place provides you with a whole picture. Each manifestation board is a visual representation, a blueprint for the success you want your life to emulate. You can create separate collages for each area of your life and hang them in the corre-sponding energy center. If you prefer, make only one board that contains all of your wishes for every area of your life (see left). As you look at it every day, the images become imprinted both consciously and subconsciously. You become what you focus on. For added enjoyment, invite friends over for a collage-making party.

the centers

The bagua has been implemented for thousands of years, and you are on the brink of making it work for you. Instead of doing all of life's work by yourself, you will be directing energy to support your endeavors. This is similar to inserting rocket boosters around your environment to give you momentum. Throughout the next several pages, you will find many solutions and enhancements to assist you in creating an exceptional life. Choose the ones that will work well in your space and feel good in your heart. Prioritize the areas of your life you wish to emphasize and begin with the corresponding centers.

As you proceed on your feng shui journey, the best advice I can give you is to take it slowly. Remember that applying the bagua is an exciting and creative process. Do not try to implement all of it overnight. Refer to the "Fast Track" for each center and start with three or four basic enhancements. Add more gradually. Be realistic and have a great time.

health and well-being—center of the bagua

Your health is your most precious possession. If your whole being is sound, you experience life with heightened vivacity and enthusiasm. The center of your home represents your physical health, your emotional and mental equilibrium, your grounding to the earth, and your spiritual connection to the universe. When you feel centered in your body, mind, and heart, you can focus clearly on creating your destiny. You need physical health in order to delight in even the simplest pleasures. You need it to enjoy a successful career, family vacations, cherished time with friends, and love with your partner and children. Self-care must be a priority. Overloading yourself with work or with social or family obligations drains your energy and diverts you from your center of well-being. It can leave you gasping for a single moment of solitude. Nourish yourself with healthy food, proper rest, meditation, nature walks, and time for love and play.

The elements for Health and Well-Being are the earth and sun. The earth represents stability and grounding; the sun gives life to everything it shines on. Your home should have a clean, vibrant, and strong center in order for

RIGHT: An abundance of fresh fruit, sunny yellow flowers, and healthy cookbooks enliven a kitchen's Health & Well-Being center.

symbol for health ——————

color—yellow ——————

energy source—flowers ——————

you to prosper. Equal amounts of serenity and power are needed for the center to thrive. Health and financial problems can arise if the center is unstable. Mark the center of your home with a plant, a stone from the earth, or the color yellow as a symbol of the sun.

health and well-being energy

Energize this center to:

Achieve more balance and harmony.

Become physically healthy.

Recover quickly from an illness.

Learn to take time for yourself.

Get focused and centered in your life.

health and well-being no-no's

Clutter, Garbage, and Dirt

You do not want your health to be contaminated, so clean up and honor your center! Wave sandalwood incense regularly to cleanse the space.

Bathrooms

Bathrooms at the center can create health and financial challenges. Refer to page 116 to energize the bathroom to the hilt. Add more than one plant to strengthen your health. Place a mirror on the outside of the bathroom door to keep healthy energy from going down the drains.

Staircases

Staircases tend to make energy move very rapidly and to travel downwards. Place heavy, solid objects at the bottom of the staircase and wrap silk vines around the banisters to slow the energy down. Hang a crystal at the top of the staircase to keep the energy from falling down to the center.

Fireplace or Stove

If the fireplace or stove is located at the center of your home, the sparks can cause instability and health problems. Calm the fire energy by placing a water element on the fireplace or next to the stove. A small water fountain or bowl of fresh water works well.

health and well-being enhancements

Here are some enhancements for this center:

- Healthy plants
- Fresh flowers
- Symbols and items from the earth such as stones, shells, ceramics, and terra-cotta pottery
- Items in yellow and green
- Paintings, symbols, or photos of the earth, sun, stars, or a sunrise
- Abundant artwork with fields of daisies, sunflowers, and yellow wild-flowers
- Real or fake fruit and vegetables in a colorful bowl
- Symbols of peace and harmony
- Photos of people who represent health and balance to you

health and well-being manifestation board

Paint or accessorize the corkboard with yellow and green. Place pictures of healthy people, natural surroundings, flowers and plants, nutritious foods, exercise regimes, spas, and calming environments. Use power words such as "Health," "Happiness," "Harmony," "Flow," "Vitality," and "Balance."

health and well-being intentional writing

Write your intentions for health and well-being. Personalize them to fit what you are trying to manifest in your life right now. Try:

"I am very happy that my health is thriving every day."

"I am excited that I have the money to go to my favorite spiritual or health retreat next month."

"I am so grateful that I create quiet time for myself every day."

"I am inspired to strengthen and nourish my body each day."

Put what you've written in a red envelope and place the envelope in a treasured box or next to a plant.

fast track to health and well-being

Immediately implement these suggestions for increased health:

Clean and clear clutter.

Add a healthy plant.

Find items in yellow and green.

Place one environmental anchor for health.

love and relationships—rear right of bagua

symbol for love

energy source—lamp

color—pink

Finding your mate is one of those extraordinary moments you look forward to from the time you are a child. When love is in your heart, it extends outward and is contagious. Attracting and enhancing the love of your life becomes easier when you exude it. The Love center reflects your relationship with a significant other and a connection with yourself. In a professional setting, this center can be used to create strong, trustworthy relationships with a business partner, client, or coworker. Thriving relationships are born and nurtured when there is reciprocity. The giving and receiving of unconditional love is a dream for each of us. If you want love, you must bestow love. When an aura of tenderness, passion, and excitement surrounds you, prospective companions will flock towards you. Communicating openly and honestly in every relationship will keep you on the right track. At the same time, you must connect inwardly by following your heart, treating yourself with kindness, and accepting love that comes your way.

The element for Love and Relationships is the earth. The earth represents grounding, stability, and receptivity. Your ability to balance a solid foundation, respect, and compassion will give a long life to all of your relationships. Have faith in the earth's ability to support you. Use this certainty as a symbol of the trust you must cultivate with your inner self and your companion. Stones, crystals, and pottery from the earth can remind you to bring balance and constancy to all of your relationships. Allow your gentle and romantic side to emerge as you energize the Love and Relationships center.

love and relationships energy
Energize this center to:

Enhance and strengthen a current relationship.

Attract a new love.

Get married.

Create more passion in your life.

Open your heart.

Improve a business relationship.

love and relationships no-no's
Bathrooms
Don't let the love in your life drain away. Implement all the suggestions

LEFT: A multitude of symbols and energy creates this bedroom's Love & Relationship center: a lamp, fresh pink roses, ceramic lovebirds, a pair of shells, a sketch of a wedding dress, candles, and the couple's happy photo. Artwork showing nuptials provides a prominent Love & Relationships anchor.

for the bathroom found on page 116. Add a pink night-light and love enhancements.

Negative or Unhappy Symbolism

Remove items from past relationships, anything with a sad memory, and lonely pictures of single people, including yourself. Avoid displaying objects that do not support a positive self-image of you as a loving, passionate, and giving person.

Fireplace

If you have a fireplace in the Love center, the sparks emanating from it may burn out a relationship. The fiery energy can provide instability. Place a water element on top of the fireplace to calm the fire. A vase of fresh flowers is the best solution.

love and relationships enhancements

Here are some enhancements for this center:

- Healthy plants
- Fresh and/or silk flowers
- Lamps or a light source with a pink bulb
- Round mirror behind a plant and/or flowers to multiply love energy
- Items in pink, peach, red, and white
- Colorful scented candles
- Pottery, stones, rose quartz, and crystals
- Silk and velvet items such as drapes, blankets, or soft pillows
- Pairs of objects such as two candles, two picture frames, two champagne glasses, or a pair of lovebirds
- Artwork with two people instead of one or three
- Environmental anchors of love such as hearts, a statue of people in love, red roses, a figurine of a bride and groom, and romantic/sensual literature, poetry, or anything that signifies love to you
- Loving photos and mementos of you and your companion on vacations and anniversaries and from your wedding and honeymoon
- Gifts and love notes from your companion
- Artwork that represents love to you
- Your favorite romantic greeting cards and/or pictures from calendars
- Photographs of island getaways and romantic cities

love and relationships manifestation board

Paint or accessorize the corkboard with red, pink, peach, or white. Place a collection of love poems, pictures of happy loving couples, romantic getaways, wedding and honeymoon ideas, pictures of couples at the altar, and photos of happily married couples you know. Add power words such as "Unconditional Love," "Open Heart," "I Receive Easily," "Passion," and "Romance."

love and relationships intentional writing

Write your intentions for Love and Relationships. Try:

"I am very happy that I am attracting a healthy, loving, and generous person into my life."

"I am so grateful that my partner supports me in my life's purpose."

"Loving people surround me wherever I go."

fast track to love and relationships

Immediately add these to enliven your loving relationships:

- Healthy plant
- Lamp with a pink bulb
- Pair of environmental anchors for love
- Romantic greeting card
- Red, pink, peach, and white items

career—front center of bagua

Finding your true calling blends what you love with the field in which you excel. Since we place so much emphasis on what we do, we sometimes lose sight of who we are. You must remember that you are not your job. However, daily work that extends out from your soul is a wonderful goal. The Career center gives you the opportunity to enhance your chosen path or occupation. Your career provides an outlet for you to express your unique talents, abilities, and brilliance. Some people are compensated financially in their work; others find spiritual fulfillment by volunteering their time.

Combining your passion with your career allows your heart to expand and creates internal alignment. Waking up with enthusiasm for your work is a goal you can achieve. You can do what you love and get paid for it, too.

Since it is common for people to change jobs and career paths many times throughout their lives, numerous opportunities are available to create a fulfilling career that is right for you. Following your dream is a journey that requires strength, courage, and persistence. Use your intuition and keep moving towards your ultimate vision.

The element for career is water. As water flows in a river, your life is a journey that drops you off at many destinations on the way to creating your destiny. You will love certain jobs and gratefully leave others behind. Keeping the flow, the circulation of healthy energy, is central to your success. You don't want water or your career to stagnate. To remind yourself, place pictures of flowing water in the Career center to enhance your progress. Shape your genuine desires into a vocation that nurtures and stimulates your soul.

career energy

Energize this center to:

Get a new job.

Receive a promotion.

Change your career path.

Create harmony in your work environment.

Grab the attention of the "higher ups."

Find stimulating volunteer work.

Discover your heart's desire.

Reveal your life's purpose.

career no-no's

Fireplace

Since water is the element for career, fire is not an ally. Place a water fountain on the fireplace and keep it running twenty-four hours a day.

Bathroom

Don't let your career go down the drain. Follow the bathroom instructions on page 116. Place a small water fountain inside the bathroom and keep it running twenty-four hours a day.

ABOVE: Water imagery distinguishes this jewelry designer's Career center. A screen showing marine life stands behind a black table displaying an array of gold, pearls, and gemstones. A blue bowl of water floats an orchid.

Make sure it sits above the toilet but not directly on top of it.

Negative Imagery

Remove items that represent jobs you disliked, unfriendly colleagues, an angry boss, a company that did not properly compensate you, or symbolism that doesn't accurately express your current or future career intentions.

career enhancements

Here are some enhancements for this center:

- Healthy plants
- Lamp or light source
- Water fountain or aquarium
- Items in black and dark blue
- Photos or paintings of moving water such as a river, stream, or calm ocean (no pictures of huge, crashing waves)
- Mirror behind plants or water fountain to double the energy
- Environmental anchors for your present or future career such as your favorite poetry books (if you want to be published), photos and albums of your favorite musicians (if you want to record), a congratulatory note on your company's stationary from the president on your grand promotion (written by you)
- Symbols and articles of volunteer groups, charity organizations, and hobbies that interest you

energy source—flowers

colors—black and blue

symbol for career

career manifestation board

Place all of your wishes for your ideal career on a corkboard. Cut out logos from companies you want to work for, photos of inspiring people who have followed their heart to a successful career, and healthy activities to complement your work schedule. Find quotes and sayings from people whose careers you respect. Include water imagery to encourage flow. Use power words such as "Motivation," "Success," "Passion," "Confidence," and "Creativity."

career intentional writing

Decide what you want to focus on in your career and affirm it in writing. Try:

"Thank you very much for sending me the best job with the appropriate salary."

"I am so grateful that my passion for drawing has brought me a terrific graphic design job for (state the amount) a year."

"My job becomes easier and more joyous every day."

"The event I am producing will be successful and profitable for everyone involved."

fast track to career

Immediately add these to energize your career:

- Healthy plant
- Light or lamp
- Water fountain
- One environmental anchor for your career
- Black and dark blue items

energy source— water fountain

symbol for wealth

colors—red and gold

wealth and prosperity—rear left of bagua

Securing financial abundance gives you the opportunity to give to others and the freedom to live out your dreams. Energizing the Wealth and Prosperity center is extremely useful because it can stimulate your investments and attract money and material possessions in new and wonderful ways. Money is energy. It is a currency exchange. You pay to receive a service or product in return. Your wealth depends on the constant ebb and flow of money in your life. Hoarding it stems from fear, which works against the principle of circulation in feng shui and closes you off to prosperity energy. If you have the proper positive attitude towards acquiring money and spending it wisely, you will invite it into your life. Let go of any negative beliefs and attitudes about people who have an abundance of money. In fact, if you bless those who may be more financially successful than you, the energy you send out will return to you. Likewise, as you energize your wealth center and become more prosperous, discover ways to give back in the process.

The element for Wealth and Prosperity is wind. As the gentle wind blows through the trees, it stirs up and spreads energy in nature. The concept of money circulating imitates the natural flow of wind and water. You should balance the amount of money going in and out. Look for the subtle and unforeseen ways you may receive money. It may show up as an unexpected tax refund or an inheritance. Acknowledge the prosperity that is already present in your life and give thanks in advance for all that is on the way.

wealth and prosperity energy

Energize this center to:

Receive a raise.

Secure a higher paying job.

Increase income to buy material items or to go on a vacation.

Finance a new project.

Raise money to live out your passion.

wealth and prosperity no-no's

Bathroom

Wealth might be draining away or going out of your life faster than it comes in. Follow the instruction for the bathroom on page 116. Add a water fountain placed higher than the toilet to increase prosperity energy. Add personal enhancements from the list below.

Clutter

Clear it so energy can move. Remove negative images and images of poverty. Throw away garbage and remove garbage cans from the actual corner. Take away broken objects or objects that depress you. Remove dead plants and flowers.

Fireplace

You do not want your money going up in flames. Place a water fountain on top of the fireplace to calm the fire or add a bowl of fresh water with gold and red marbles or stones. A vase of fresh flowers works, too. Any object that holds water will tame the flames.

wealth and prosperity enhancements

Here are some enhancements for this center:

- Large healthy plants
- Water fountain or aquarium running twenty-four hours a day (except at night in your bedroom)
- Lamps, night-light, or other light source with a red light bulb
- Red and gold items and accent colors of green and purple
- Mirror behind a plant or water element to "double" prosperity energy

- Environmental anchors of wealth such as faux million dollar bills, miniature dream cars, gold bowl with real or fake coins, Chinese money Buddha, and actual cash in the center
- Real or silk flowers in red and gold
- Valuable possessions such as sculptures, crystal, and precious antiques
- Artwork with vibrant colors and prosperity imagery with an abundance of items such as many trees or a field of flowers

wealth and prosperity manifestation board

Paint or accessorize a corkboard in the colors of red and gold. Add pictures, photos, quotes, and affirmations representing all your dreams and wishes for prosperity, wealth, and abundance. Ideas include dream cars, homes, boats, planes, vacations, and jewelry. Add power words such as "Wealth," "Success," "Abundance," and "Generosity."

wealth and prosperity intentional writing

Write your wishes for Wealth and Prosperity. Try:

"I am very happy; my wealth increases every day."

"I am so grateful for the raise of $20,000 by January."

"Thank you for the money to go to Tahiti this summer."

"It is fantastic that I can easily finance my children's college education."

fast track to wealth and prosperity

Immediately add these to multiply your wealth and prosperity:

- Large healthy plant
- Water fountain or aquarium bubbling twenty-four hours a day
- Light source with a red bulb
- One environmental anchor for wealth
- Red and gold items

water fountains galore

The three best centers for water fountains are Wealth and Prosperity, Career, and Helpful People. However, if you only want one in your home, the Wealth and Prosperity center is the most beneficial and profitable. Remember to keep water fountains running twenty-four hours a day, except in your bedroom when you sleep. This will calm the energy for a good night's rest.

 # family—middle left of bagua

You are the embodiment of those who have come before you. Your grand-parents and great grandparents passed down a heritage to you along with their genes, habits, thought patterns, and material possessions. The Family center represents your roots—past, present, and future. It can uplift the relationship with your parents, siblings, aunts, uncles, and cousins. You can recognize where you came from and notice how much you have evolved.

You should respect and love your family, but if they are not kind, you do not have to spend time with them. Embrace the good qualities and release the undesirable ones. In addition, the Family center encompasses the dear people who feel like family, including friends, neighbors, and adopted parents. Health is also a major component of Family. If your relationships with family and friends are nurturing and strong, you are healthier physi-cally, emotionally, and mentally. Your health prospers with a solid founda-tion of love surrounding you.

ABOVE: Happy photographs of parents and grandparents are ideal in the Family center. The green wood frames create family harmony, and flowers beautify and energize relationships.

The element for Family is thunder. When family comes together, an electric charge sparks love, conflict, jealousy, communication, and unity. Yearly reunions are never dull. You learn honesty, grow emotionally, become compassionate, create boundaries, and develop strong bonds. It is common to experience stormy conditions within the family unit. Sometimes a little thunder and lightning can disintegrate negative energy between family members. This can be a wake up call to forgive. When the commotion has settled, you need to let go of resentments. Forgiving allows your heart to open and attracts nurturing people into your life. Your ability to forgive, be present, and reside in gratitude will keep you healthy and happy.

energy source—flowers

color—green

symbol for family

family energy

Energize this center to:

Create open and honest family communication.

Forgive and heal an upset with family.

Send love and sweetness to family.

Attract strong, healthy friendships.

Honor your ancestors or heritage.

Become emotionally grounded and physically healthy.

family no-no's

Negative Family Imagery

Remove photos of people who have been judgmental, antiques inherited from relatives who were argumentative and upset, gifts that drain your energy, and anything you are displaying out of guilt.

Dead Objects

Only living energy belongs in the Family center. Remove dead plants, dried flowers, preserved butterflies and insects, and ashes of the deceased. Rid your house of all dead things.

family enhancements

Here are some enhancements for this center:

- Healthy plants
- Fresh and silk flowers in bright colors
- Wood objects including bookcases, frames, sculptures, lamps, bowls, and bamboo
- Green items and blue as an accent color

- Pictures or photos of green pastures, lush trees, the rain forest, gardens, and landscapes
- Photos of cherished family and friends at happy occasions
- Environmental anchors for family such as beautiful heirlooms, china, stemware, jewelry, or mementos from loved ones
- Symbols and photos of health, vibrancy, and strength

family manifestation board

Paint or accessorize the corkboard with green and blue. Place photos of happy family occasions, revered family members you want to emulate, photos and articles of famous loving families, photos of good friends, hearty people doing healthy activities, healing environments, nature imagery, plants, and trees. Find quotes dealing with family values, morals, and health. Use power words such as "Honesty," "Communication," "Forgiveness," and "Love."

family intentional writing

Write exactly what you desire in terms of your family. Try:

"I am so grateful that I easily forgive my mother and father and open my heart to them."

"I am excited that my birthday celebration is full of good friends, loving family, and tons of acknowledgment."

"Thank you for the complete healing my grandfather is experiencing right now, allowing him to live in peace and ease."

"I triumphantly follow in the footsteps of my most successful and fulfilled ancestors."

fast track to family

Immediately add these to strengthen your family:

- Healthy plant
- Happy photos of family and friends in wooden frames
- Green items
- One environmental anchor for family

creativity and children—middle right of bagua

The creative impulse inside of you yearns to spread its wings. Imagine the implications of bottling the combined creativities of Michelangelo, da Vinci, Mozart, and Shakespeare and pouring them into your soul. How would it manifest through you? Creation is the art of bringing the unseen into the visible world. You give birth to creative projects in the same way one gives birth to a child. This energy center symbolizes your creative pursuits and your children. A child's creativity is boundless. Adults would be wise to emulate their imagination and wonderment. Remind yourself to be as playful, spontaneous, and exuberant as children. If you have children, you can enhance this area for their well-being, schooling, and relationships. Sing, dance, play games, and invite your children to join the fun and express themselves in a joyful way.

The lake is the element associated with creativity. The beauty of the lake can inspire you. When you see your true reflection clearly, you can dive into a lake of wondrous possibilities. As your creativity reflects your image, so do your children. Remember what you were passionate about as a child or teenager and dip into that creative reservoir. This center encourages you to bring your artistic abilities, musical talents, and hobbies to the forefront. Allow your passions, which no one needs to understand or agree with, to emerge and materialize. Your creativity allows you to shape situations, ideas, events, and projects in a unique and marvelous way. Invite your own inner child to run free and to create with an open heart. Stimulate your creative juices in as many ways as possible.

creativity and children energy
Energize this center to:

Successfully embark on a new creative project.

Express more creativity.

Get "unstuck."

Become pregnant.

Increase your child's learning skills.

Improve your relationship with your children.

LEFT: Let your imagination run wild in the Creativity & Children center. An art space equipped with easel, paints, brushes, and art books facilitate the creative flow. Yellow tulips bring life and energy to you and your children.

symbol for creativity

energy source—flowers

color—white and pastels

creativity and children no-no's

Clutter

Clutter keeps you bogged down and unable to access your higher inspirations. Dispose of it to unlock your creative expression and to get your positive energy flowing. Your children will benefit as well.

Negative Symbols

Remove items that represent creative mishaps, photos of people who do not support your creative endeavors, and your child's unsuccessful projects.

creativity and children enhancements

Here are some enhancements for this center:

- Healthy plants
- Lamps or light source
- Objects such as candleholders, electronic equipment, and picture frames made of copper, silver, pewter, gold, brass, and other metals
- White items and pastels as accent colors
- Childlike toys, games, and stuffed animals
- Arts and crafts supplies such as paints, crayons, and colored paper
- Music and musical instruments
- Environmental anchors for creativity such as prints from a favorite artist, a sculpture, photos of creative geniuses like Mozart, poetry, and handmade arts and crafts
- Baby items such as pictures of newborns, baby books, baby blankets, and baby pillows as environmental anchors to encourage pregnancy
- Your child's artwork, good report cards, drawings, and projects

creativity and children manifestation board

Paint or accessorize your corkboard in white with pastel accents. Place a collection of your wildest creative endeavors along with clippings from magazines showing inspirational poetry, music, child prodigies, and babies. Find quotes and photos of creative people you admire. Place symbols or your most successful creative projects on the manifestation board. Add power words such as "Inspiration," "Childlike," "Playful," "Creative Expression," and "Fertility."

creativity and children intentional writing

Affirm your children's creative desires and your own in writing. Try:

"I am ecstatic that my creativity is pouring out into all my projects."

"I am so grateful that I will deliver a healthy child this year."

"My playful and childlike qualities inspire me to experiment without having to be perfect."

"My child becomes more intelligent, loving, and expressive every day."

fast track to creativity and children

Immediately add these to enhance your creativity and children:

- Healthy plant
- Lamp
- One environmental anchor for creativity or for children
- White items

knowledge and wisdom—front left of bagua

Knowledge provides you with an abundance of opportunities. Your thirst for knowledge and wisdom keeps your mind active, engages your brain muscles, and expands the scope of your world. Learning something new every day stimulates and sensitizes you to the life force that surrounds you. The Knowledge and Wisdom center deals with higher education and inner contemplation. Learning broadens your perspective and opens your mind to new cultures, traditions, technologies and ways of living. You can gain enlightenment from books, teachers, schooling, film, television, spiritual practice, and your inner guidance. This center can also enhance your children's education and learning abilities.

Gathering useless information is very different from obtaining knowledge that nurtures you and your family. Learning new ideas, concepts, and techniques keeps you humble and grounded. You should respect the teachers and mentors who came before you. Building upon their accomplishments saves you time, energy, and error. You don't need to reinvent the wheel. The universe has infinite knowledge; only you can choose to tap into it.

The element for Knowledge and Wisdom is mountain. The image of wise people coming down from the mountains to share their knowledge and understanding of the universe is recognized all over the world. The quiet of the mountain allows you to still the mind, clear the clutter of everyday

RIGHT: Blue should be prominent in the Knowledge & Wisdom center. A bookcase brimming with Asian artifacts, a healthy plant, some books and a lamp symbolizing knowledge can energize you on the path to enlightenment.

symbol for knowledge

color—blue

energy source—plant

stress, and get in touch with the authentic part of yourself. When you get away from it all, you can access your inner guidance and discover your relation to the rest of the world. You are able to look at situations in terms of the bigger picture. How can you incorporate the insights found on the mountain into your real life? Meditation and focused breathing will bring you closer to the divine spark within you.

knowledge and wisdom center energy
Energize this center to:

Gain greater knowledge in a new area.

Become a better student.

Inspire your children to study.

Quiet your mind.

Expand the process of self-discovery.

Start meditating

knowledge and wisdom no-no's
Clutter
You must not clutter your space and mind with useless items. A clear head is necessary to absorb knowledge correctly and rapidly. Now is a perfect time to clear out your bookshelves.

Negative Symbols
Remove photos and books of people who do not emulate wisdom and perception. Do not allow old newspapers and magazine to pile up because they can bombard you with information that blocks your own inner guidance.

knowledge and wisdom enhancements
Here are some enhancements for this center:
- Healthy plants
- Light, lamps, and candles to become "enlightened"
- Deep blue and green items
- Books, tapes, and videos you are currently studying or wish to study
- Environmental anchors of wisdom such as photos and

paintings of people like Einstein, Gandhi, Buddha, your grandmother, self-help motivational speakers, or smart animals such as dolphins
- Artwork depicting images of mountains or quiet places such as gardens or beaches
- Meditation objects such as a pillow, shawl, altar, or spiritual music
- Fresh or silk flowers
- Water fountain to energize the knowledge of how to access wealth, fame, success, and love

knowledge and wisdom manifestation board

Paint or accessorize a corkboard with the colors blue and green. Fill it with everything you want to learn to incorporate into your life. Include people you would love to learn from or a picture of a brilliant person whose mind you'd like to borrow. Also include retreats and seminars you want to attend and spiritual pilgrimages you want to make. Add a picture of mountains such as the Himalayas or Machu Picchu, and/or pages from catalogues of schools or night classes you would like to attend. Include quotes from noted scholars or other intelligent people. Add power words such as "Brilliance," "Enlightenment," and "Inner Knowing."

knowledge and wisdom intentional writing

Place your intentions for acquiring wisdom in writing. Try:

"I am so grateful that I easily absorb and retain the information necessary to succeed in my job."

"I am excited that I have been accepted into my chosen program at my desired university."

"Inner knowledge and wisdom are revealed to me when I listen with an open heart."

"I am thrilled that I have the opportunity and finances to participate in a meditation retreat this summer."

fast track to knowledge and wisdom

Immediately add these to enhance your knowledge and wisdom:

- Healthy plant
- Lamp
- Blue candles
- Environmental anchor for knowledge

fame and reputation—rear center of bagua

How do you present yourself to the world? What are you known for? Every day, the actions, behaviors, words, and energy you exude shape the way people view you. Regardless of what has transpired in your past, you now have the opportunity to create a new perception of yourself. The Fame and Reputation center is associated with your character and image. You should embellish this center if you want to gain respect at home, work, or in the community. You can transform your reputation and become recognized for something new. For example, a mother of three also wants to be known for her career in photography, or a businessman who is a world traveler desires to settle down so he is recognized for being a good father. Become clear about how you want to be seen before you energize the center. Traditionally, stimulating the Fame center can propel you into the spotlight.

The element for Fame and Reputation is fire. Fire illuminates you and your unique characteristics and accomplishments. The flames spark new ideas and aspirations. They motivate you to move in a new direction. The fiery energy projects you into the limelight; media and people will take notice. When someone is referred to as "on fire," it usually means they are succeeding in a tremendous way. They are at the height of their potential. Place appropriate symbolic objects to create a spectacular outcome: fireplaces, candles, lights, and lamps can be powerful energizers. Your reputation is defined over time, and it requires strong intention to transform it. Cultivate honorable virtues so you can sincerely shine them outward. The more you "walk the talk," the faster your new fame and reputation will manifest.

fame and reputation energy
Energize this center to:

Gain recognition at home, work, or in the community.

Publicize or promote yourself in a new way.

Win the respect you deserve.

Become famous for something unique.

Create a plan for how people will view you in the future.

fame and reputation no-no's
Bathroom
You don't want to have your fame in the toilet. Implement all suggestions to

energize the bathroom on page 116. However, do not hang crystals over the drains if the bathroom is located in Fame. Add a night-light with red bulb and keep it on twenty-four hours a day. Burn red candles when in the bathroom.

Water

Water puts out the fire. Remove any water fountains or movable water elements from this center and move them to the Wealth or Career center. Avoid symbols of water, rain, snow, ocean, lake, or rivers.

Negative Symbols

Remove all symbols in objects, photos, art, and books that do not represent how you want to be known now and in the future. Clear away items representing people or situations with negative, crooked, or questionable reputations.

fame and reputation enhancements

Here are some enhancements for this center:

- Tall, healthy plants
- Standing lamp, night-light, or lamp that shoots red light up to the ceiling
- Red items and orange, yellow, and green accents
- Fireplace, candles, and lanterns
- Artwork and pictures of the sun, fire, and fireworks
- Objects of recognition such as diplomas, endorsements, trophies, university credentials, prizes, certificates of appreciation or valor from work, the community, or family
- Television or radio to symbolize your fame being broadcast all over the world
- Environmental anchors of people you admire and want to emulate such as respected teachers, authors, performers, business people, powerful corporations, celebrities, and anyone you respect and admire and with whom you wish to be identified

fame and reputation manifestation board

Paint or accessorize your corkboard with red. Create a collage of how you would like to be seen in the world. Add photos and quotes of people you admire, projects you want to be involved in, and illustrations of how you want to look physically. Add power words and phrases such as "Respect," "Admiration," "Leader," and "Internationally Known."

color—red

symbol for fame

energy source—flowers

RIGHT: A missing Fame & Reputation center is brought back into the bagua with an outdoor fireplace. The red accents from the candles, lampshades, and seat cushions attract attention while the flowers enhance your good reputation.

LEFT: A serene wall hanging complements a meditative Buddha in the Helpful People center. Any symbol representing spiritual guidance is ideal for this area—especially important is a box holding your requests to the seen and unseen Helpful People in your life. Fresh flowers and a lucky bamboo plant generate beneficial energy.

fame and reputation intentional writing

Write your intentions for how you desire to be known in the present and future. Try:

"I am so grateful that I am recognized for my work."

"I am ecstatic that my good name and projects have positive reviews in newspaper and magazine articles."

"I am thrilled that I am known internationally as a philanthropist."

"Thank you for the amazing opportunity to appear as a guest on a national television show."

fast track to fame and reputation

Immediately add these suggestions to uplift your good reputation:

- Large, healthy plant
- Lamp with red bulb
- Two red candles
- Environmental anchor for fame and reputation

helpful people—front right of bagua

energy source—plant

symbol for helpful people

color—black

If you were granted the opportunity to create a circle of any ten people (living, deceased, or mythical) to advise and help you to fulfill your dreams, who would be on the list? You might invite one specializing in the each significant area of your life including love, inspiration, strength, health, spirituality, ambition, wealth, intelligence, psychology, and laughter. Would you select Mother Theresa or the Dalai Lama? How about Einstein, Lucille Ball, Gandhi, Babe Ruth, and Aphrodite? The Helpful People center represents those who mentor, guide, and assist you. They are the ones who give you physical, mental, emotional, and spiritual support and insight. They may be people you are acquainted with or famous people you don't know but from whom you'd like guidance. Helpful people can include your family, friends, spiritual counselor, real estate agent, landlord, plumber, employees, or clients. When you need assistance with anything in your life, energize this center!

The element for Helpful People is heaven. Guidance and answers can come from the spirit world. Many times angels from heaven show up as helpful guides to shed light or aid you when you need them most.

Sometimes they are random people at the supermarket or on the beach. They say or do something spectacular that moves your life forward in a huge way. Symbols and pictures of heaven, angels, sky, sun, religious items, and your spiritual mentors placed in this center increase your connection with Helpful People. Remember to offer assistance to others as you ask for guidance in your life. Synchronicity and good luck occur when you are prepared and in the right place at right time.

helpful people energy

Energize this center to:

Bring more helpful people, clients, investors, and mentors into your life.

Develop your inner guidance and intuition.

Attract the right people to help or teach you.

Find an experienced person so that you can delegate some responsibilities.

Increase synchronicity in your life.

helpful people no-no's

Clutter and Garbage

You need to have a clean space for energy, intuition, guidance, and good luck to flow in and around. If you are bogged down in the minutia of clutter, you might not notice when a helpful person is standing in front of you.

Bathrooms

You do not want your helpful people disappearing down the drains. Follow the suggestions for bathrooms on page 116. Keep the energy high since the element is heaven. You might want to paint the ceiling to look like the sky or hang a plant from the ceiling.

Negative Images

Remove items or photos of people that hinder your progress by depleting your energy or getting in the way of your dreams.

helpful people enhancements

Here are some enhancements for this center:

- Healthy Plants
- Light or lamps
- Water fountain
- Gray, silver, or black and white items

- Inspiring artwork that portrays heaven, angels, spirit, nature, spiritual teachers, saints, and respected role models
- Photographs, symbols, articles, and books of helpful people in the world
- Representations of the corporations you want to work for, magazines you want to interview you, wealthy people you want to sponsor you, and mentors you want to coach you
- The name of the person you want help from and your request
- A special box to hold your requests
- Spiritual environmental anchors that symbolize your spiritual connection

helpful people manifestation board

Paint or accessorize your corkboard with gray and silver. Place pictures, symbols, and images of the Helpful People in your life on the board. Who are you asking for help right now? Is it your lawyer, sister, accountant, housekeeper, or friend? Include everyone and everything you receive guidance from including nature and spiritual elements. Write power words such as "Guidance," "Gratitude," and "Synchronicity."

helpful people intentional writing

Write your specific desires for help and support. Try:

"I am grateful that my landlord lowered my rent to $800 a month."

"I am excited that my brother is watching the kids this weekend."

"I am thankful that I am being guided and protected every day."

"Synchronicity shows up in my life at exactly the right moment."

fast track to helpful people

Immediately add these to increase the helpful people in your life:

- Healthy plant
- Lamp or night-light
- Environmental anchor of past, present, and future helpful people
- Gray, silver, and black and white items

Intentional writing is essential. Ask for help from specific people in writing and include a picture or article about them.

seven:

the front entrance and foyer

Traveling from room to room in the following four chapters, you will create beauty and harmony, and you'll also program your home to support you. As with every feng shui consultation, the best place to begin is the front entrance. Working your way through your home, you will find the most favorable recommendations for each room.

I encourage you to implement a few changes immediately. This will allow you to experience how shifting the energy transforms a room so that it looks and feels better. Taking action is the key.

Using your intuition, decide which areas require the most attention and begin with them. Take baby steps. Set out to improve one corner, table, or arrangement and work your way through the area. Revitalizing your space should be fun. For added pleasure, you can invite friends and family to partake in the feng shui activities. The point is to enjoy the process, whether it takes one month or one year.

PREVIOUS PAGE: Grand, arched wooden doors create a powerful and grounded entrance to this magnificent Spanish-influenced home. Potted palms uplift and soften the downward energy exerted by exposed beams, and the red roses provide a burst of color as energy moves into the house.

RIGHT: If you regularly enter your home through a side door, treat it like a formal entrance by adding lush plants and colorful flowers. Your entrance should offer a warm welcome to you and opportunities.

the front entrance

The entrance to your home is considered the mouth of your dwelling, thus making it one of the most important factors for actively drawing in positive energy. In the same way you nourish your body with healthy food, you must fuel your surroundings with beneficial energy. The amount of healthy living energy you can bring in the front door makes a huge difference in the overall feng shui of your space. The question to ask is, "How can I encourage health, prosperity, abundance, and tranquility to appear in my life right now?"

The first step is to create a clear, open, and beautiful entrance for energy to move through and to circulate in your home. When your entrance radiates positive energy, it opens the door to your destiny. Feng shui promotes the belief that your golden opportunities come in through the front door. Think of the door as your official welcoming committee. It is the threshold for all good things to come your way.

You should embellish the formal entrance since it is ordinarily seen from the street and maintains your public image. However, it is possible that you don't use this entrance on a daily basis. The door you do use most frequently is significant in allowing the majority of the outside energy to flow inside the home. So, if you enter through an alternate door such as a laundry room, garage, or side door, you must evaluate and beautify it with the same verve as you would the formal entrance.

first impressions

Your front entrance creates a first impression for you, for others, and for unlimited opportunities to come your way. It sets the intention for the rest of your home. Every time you drive up, your house either emanates an aura of success, abundance, and pride, or a feeling of disarray, laziness, and misfortune. When you are on vacation and drive up to a hotel entrance, what immediately goes through your mind? You look at the maintenance of the building, landscaping, cars in the parking lot, and other indicators. You make dozens of evaluations instantaneously. You are either elated with your travel agent or massively disappointed. When the hotel driveway welcomes you with beautiful trees, colorful flowers, a grand water fountain, and a smiling doorman, you are content before you have even stepped into the lobby.

In the same way, your home must welcome you, your guests, and all of your opportunities with loving, open arms. Before these "opportunities" ring the doorbell, your goal is to flood them with beauty, happiness, and comfort. While they wait for you to answer the door, give them multiple reasons to generate positive thoughts about you. Create a home that shimmers and stands out from the rest.

Entrance Exam

Step outside your door. What do you see? Does the outside of your home emanate beauty? Notice the upkeep of the paint, roof, and landscaping. A home that is clean and well cared for leaves a lasting impression. The trees, shrubs, and flowers should be thriving and well trimmed. The path

ABOVE: Placing chairs on your front porch both symbolically and practically invites your guests to feel at home. The bouquet of pink roses and flowering plants give a wonderful first impression —a preview to the care and charm waiting inside.

leading up to the home must be easily accessible. Clear away bicycles, trash, garbage bins, dead plants, newspapers, water bottles, and broken sprinklers.

Turn around to survey your street, neighbors, and community. Healthy energy must surround you. If freeway traffic is bombarding your ears or large oppressive buildings are looming above you, you must deflect their disturbing energy away from your home. Don't allow unfinished projects in the yard to deplete you. Complete them so you can arrive home to comfort and ease. For just a moment, step outside yourself and judge your home. What kind of person would you say lives here?

home protection

In feng shui, you must regulate the type and speed of energy entering your home. You only want to invite nourishing energy inside. If your house has power, then everything within it has power. Fifty percent of good feng shui relies on the amount of positive energy flowing into your home through doors and windows, while the other fifty percent is generated by the proper arrangement and specific energizers you supply within the environment.

Outside the front door are various types of energy you need to assess. Certain kinds you want to encourage, and others you want to diffuse. Healthy energy should move easily, gently, and continuously into the home; harmful energy should be repelled, reflected, and minimized. Feng shui offers potent solutions to protect your home in order to avoid misfortune, health problems, and missed opportunities.

In the next section, you will start the process by determining if your home needs protection. If it does, implement the necessary solutions. Afterwards, you can strengthen the positive energy by incorporating the "Outdoor Enhancements."

LEFT: Abundant foliage in the front yard is a natural solution for diffusing negative energy coming towards the door. In all other cases, keep trees and shrubs well trimmed so they do not block positive energy entering the home.

unfavorable energy

According to the principles of feng shui, the following adverse sites can cause problems when located opposite your main door. If you just discovered that you have one of these situations, don't fret. Remember that you have already inhabited your space for a certain period of time, so things can only improve. Use your intuition to choose the solution that feels right for you. You may implement all of the solutions to maximize the deflection of negative energy or any one of them to fit your home's style.

Once you understand the different types of unfavorable energy and the solutions, you can create good feng shui on your own. For example, imagine you live on the twenty-third floor of a high-rise building. Your kitchen window looks directly towards a hospital. Since you cannot plant trees outside the twenty-third floor, simply hang a plant in the window to disperse the unhealthy energy and to block the view. You could also hang a mirror in the window with the reflective side pointing toward the hospital. Experiment to learn which solutions feel best.

Churches, Hospitals, Police Stations, Cemeteries, and Funeral Homes

Energy originating from these sites can cause vulnerability when situated next to or across from your home. Some of the energy implications caused by excess grief, death, disease, and crime can activate depression, illness, fears, disharmony, and possible financial loss to the household. You must block the view and the energy simultaneously.

Railroads, Freeways, and Airports

Enormous amounts of energy are generated by these thoroughfares. If they are situated very close to the home, the racing energy can cause fear and anxiety. Trees will slow down energy and block views of railroads and freeways. Installing a water fountain can partially drown out the unsettling noises.

Cul-de-sacs, Dead Ends, and T-Junctions

You must redirect the energy if your home is located in one of these situations. If you open your door and look down a long narrow street, you must deflect the arrow-like energy pointing at your home. If the energy is not diverted, you may experience financial loss, illness, divorce, and general misfortune. Foliage will slow down energy and minimize your vulnerability to the fast-moving stream.

Electrical Stations and Telephone Poles

The electromagnetic frequencies generated by high voltage electricity can cause mental and emotional problems, insomnia, and health difficulties. The electromagnetic voltage interferes with the natural energy field of the home and the people living inside.

Solutions for Above-Listed Unfortunate Sites

- Place a convex mirror above your door and hang a wind chime in front of the entrance.
- Set a gazing ball on a stand next to your door to deflect greater amounts of negative energy.
- For added protection, plant healthy bushes or small trees in front of your property, near the sidewalk, to obstruct the view from an unfortunate site. Do not plant them close to the door because they will block beneficial energy from entering your home.
- Install a light fixture above the door to uplift the energy.

Sharp Corners

Sharp corners from neighbors' rooftops, garages, balconies, and buildings can shoot arrow-like energy into the house. This piercing energy can affect health and finances.

Columns and Pillars

Columns and pillars that have sharp edges may affect health and finances. Round pillars that do not obstruct the entrance are better. Make sure that they are not too big or too close to the door.

Solutions for Sharp Corners, Columns, and Pillars

- Grow live vines or wrap silk vines around sharp objects or corners.
- Hang a wind chime between the sharp edge and the door to reflect the piercing energy.
- Round the edges of all sharp corners.

energy for the front entrance

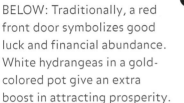

BELOW: Traditionally, a red front door symbolizes good luck and financial abundance. White hydrangeas in a gold-colored pot give an extra boost in attracting prosperity.

After you implement feng shui solutions to protect your space, you'll want to uplift and maximize the beneficial energy gliding into your home. Create a sanctuary of light and joy by adding color, living energy, and pizzazz to your entrance. Your goal is to feel excited to come home every day.

Decide what or whom you wish to invite into your home and life. If you desire love, create a sensual and romantic front entrance with fragrant flowers. For a new career, install a water fountain to circulate opportunities around you. If you want increased prosperity, paint your door red and place plants in expensive-looking gold pots next to the entrance. Have fun and get creative; try using gold spray paint on an existing planter that could use a facelift. Become clear about your intentions and goals; make a powerful statement and actively pursue them.

In feng shui, a red front door is very fortunate. It calls attention and uplifts the energy and opportunities coming through your door. A gold door calls in prosperity and reminds you of the treasure that is waiting for you inside. A green door symbolizes money, health, and nature; purple calls in spiritual energies. Take each enhancement one step at a time. Creating good feng shui is a continuous process. Prioritize your most important changes, make a schedule, and allow your house to evolve as you do.

the bagua and your property

In order to apply the principles of feng shui to your property, place the bagua on your entire plot of land in the same way as with your home. Use the formal entrance to the lot as the "front door." As you view the property from the street, your Knowledge and Wisdom, Career, and Helpful People centers will be closest to the sidewalk. The Wealth and Prosperity, Fame and Reputation, and Love and Relationships centers will be in the backyard at the rear of the property. Use your creativity to mold the enhancements in chapter six to fit an outdoor setting. Here are a few suggestions to get you started. You can embellish your Love and Relationships center with a romantic gazebo or a petite table for two. A beautiful waterfall is well situated in the Wealth and Prosperity, Career, or Helpful People centers. A tree house, dollhouse, or jungle gym for the kids is a great addition to the Children and Creativity center. The Family center is a perfect spot to put a picnic table for summer dinners. A barbecue or outdoor stove can ignite your Fame and Reputation center. Finally, a bench or chaise lounge for quiet reading can be placed in Knowledge and Wisdom. Remember that the front yard symbolizes your present life, and the back yard represents your future. Improve the overall feng shui of the property by removing the weeds and debris and, of course, by planting healthy trees and plants.

TOP RIGHT: Installing a fountain in the Career, Wealth, or Helpful People centers of the property is a good idea.

BOTTOM RIGHT: For increased good fortune, overlay the bagua on your property; colors and symbols associated with centers can assist you in landscaping.

meandering pathways

If the walkway from the street to your front door is a straight line, you must disperse fast-moving energy shooting towards the entrance. To avoid an overwhelming current, plant flowers and bushes along the edge of the footpath. You may also hang a wind chime in front of the entrance. In general, gently curving pathways leading towards the door are recommended because energy can travel along them at an even pace.

outdoor enhancements

The following is a list of feng shui enhancements that will strengthen and uplift the energy coming into your front door. Feel free to implement as many as you want. Mix and match those that bring the maximum energy and beauty to your specific outdoor environment.

Trees, Bushes, Potted Plants, and Flowers

Elements of nature are terrific for creating new growth, healing, harmony, and energy to all aspects of your life. People feel expansive and joyful in nature because of the abundance of oxygen and living energy. The natural beauty of colorful flowers, especially a powerful red, invigorates the energy pouring into the home. All trees and bushes should be well manicured to keep from blocking the energy and light flowing into the house. Remove all dead plants and leaves.

Enhancements

- To soften and slow down energy along a straight walkway, plant brightly colored flowers and shrubs along the edge, guiding you to the front door.
- Place a tall, healthy plant in a red or gold pot on either side of your doorstep for wealth. They should not block the entrance.
- Plant a tree where a corner of the home is missing. This tree creates stability and establishes energy for the missing center of the bagua.
- Soften pillars and columns by hanging plants and flowers around the sharp edges.
- Plant pine trees in your yard to symbolize resilience and integrity; plant bamboo for wisdom and longevity; use fruit trees including apple, orange, and pomegranate for luck, joy, and fertility.

Water Features

Water fountains, birdbaths, lakes, ponds, and streams are considered lucky elements in front of your home and in your backyard. Since water is aligned with money, prosperity, and abundance, be sure the water flows towards your home. Moving water equates to thriving finances, forward movement in your career, abundant health, and happiness. Ensure that your water does not become stagnant and dirty. Healthy energy is always circulating.

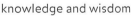

wealth and prosperity

fame and reputation

love and relationships

family

health and well-being

creativity and children

knowledge and wisdom

career

helpful people

Enhancements

- Install a water fountain on the right side of the main door to bring fortunate energy in every time you open the door.
- Place a circular water fountain in the middle of the front yard. Surround it with plants and flowers for success in your career or to counteract a T-junction or cul-de-sac.
- Design a round or oval fishpond in the rear left area of your backyard to stimulate finances.
- Install a water feature in the front or backyard to complete a missing corner or energy center.
- According to the bagua of your property, place water elements in Career, Wealth, and Helpful People energy centers for good fortune.

Natural Light and Lamps

Light aligns itself with fire, activating everything it encounters. Light attracts attention, brightens your emotional outlook, motivates you, and empowers your health, wealth, and fame. Allow an abundance of natural sunlight into your house through doors and windows. The sun's energy sustains the world.

Enhancements

- Keep a bright light on above your door twenty-four hours a day. Use a 100-watt pink bulb. If you need to save electricity, turn it on for at least a few hours a day.
- Install a lamppost in the yard to stabilize and energize a missing center.
- If your house is below street level, place spotlights in the rear of the backyard pointing towards the roof. Shining the light at least four hours a day can remedy loss of money or career difficulties.
- Hang red or white lights around your front porch to attract attention to golden opportunities.

Welcome Signs, Mats, and Statues

Create a doorstep that engenders positive thoughts, warm feelings, excitement, passion, and genuine hospitality. Welcome yourself, your friends, your colleagues, and all your opportunities into your home.

Enhancements

- Buy a colorful welcome mat. Imagine that the moment visitors step onto it, their love for you is heightened.

LEFT: An enchanting waterfall and koi pond energize the Career center in this front yard.

- Hang a welcome sign or symbol at eye level. Select one that inspires you. For instance, hang a beautiful photograph, an uplifting quote, a silk flower wreath, or any item that brings a smile to your face.
- Place a statue to bring stability and protection to your home. This can be a ceramic angel, a friendly animal, or a cultural or religious artifact such as a stone Buddha. Any personal environmental anchor at the entrance will remind you of your goals and desires.

the garage

Since every area is meaningful in feng shui, treat your garage as you would any other room of your house. If you enter through your garage on a daily basis, it serves as your entrance. Make sure you protect the opening to your garage in the same way you would your front door since the majority of outside energy will flow in through it. It should be decorated and energized in accordance with the rest of your home. If the garage is clean and organized, it can provide a wonderful area to embark on creative projects for the entire family.

The garage is considered part of the overall bagua if it is attached to the home and an internal door leads you directly inside. Many times, either the Knowledge and Wisdom or Helpful People center is located in the garage. Embellish it with the correct colors and enhancements as indicated in chapter 6. Have fun and look forward to driving in and out every day.

Enhancements
- Place a gazing ball directly outside of your garage door to disperse negative energy that may travel towards your home from an unfortunate site
- Set up shelves to organize your storage items. Hanging a curtain to hide the shelving will add color and movement.

your car

If your car is a mess, you'll have a difficult time feeling successful, focused, and confident. Treat yourself to car washes and clear the clutter. Add colorful floor mats and a fresh fragrance. Listen to motivational speakers and books on tape. Select a favorite mug to place in the drink holder. Keep bottled water close by for constant hydration. Use the time you spend in your car wisely. Learn, grow, and drive joyfully.

take action now

The following are five practical suggestions for outside your home.

1. **Remove** weeds, dead plants, garbage, and old newspapers from the yard and doorstep.

2. **Assess the area for unfavorable energy** and determine if it requires a mirror, gazing ball, or wind chime.

3. **Place a tall plant** in a colorful pot on either side of the front door. A tall plant raises the energy; smaller ones keep the energy low.

4. **Browse through cherished** greeting cards or magazines for a pleasing picture or quote to use as a temporary welcome sign.

5. **Sketch the appearance** of your ideal main entrance and garage including the environmental anchors you will use to help materialize your specific goals.

- Paint the walls and/or the floor a vibrant color.
- Add silk plants and flowers to bring in energy from nature.
- Install indoor/outdoor carpeting to the areas that surround your car.
- Hang inspirational art or posters on the walls.
- Place a welcome sign in the garage. Greet yourself with an inspirational photo or saying that makes you smile.

the foyer

The foyer makes a statement about you. It is a preview of the rest of your home and an extension of the first impression established by the main entrance. Your artwork, furniture, and passions are displayed here for the world to see. As favorable energy enters your home, it clears and rotates the negative aspects out of your life to allow positive ones to move in. Making tangible changes in the visible appearance of the foyer can immediately result in a transformation of attitude, well-being, and success. After being out all day, stepping inside your home can be a delight or an upset depending on the condition of your foyer.

As you make practical alterations in the physical template of your home, you begin to bring about inner change. The more positive and life affirming your environment is, the easier it becomes to expand your visions and manifest your desires. People are creatures of habit; simply move objects around and new energy responses are stimulated immediately.

If you crave transformation, you must change your thoughts, your actions, and your surroundings. For example, place a vase with fresh red and pink roses on an entry table to inspire love.

BELOW: An entry table's peaceful Buddhas, bright red flowers, and special books serve as environmental anchors in the foyer.

If you wish to live a more spiritual existence, put a photo of a sacred site or spiritual teacher inside the main door. For organization, a beautiful tray or hook for your keys eliminates last minute searches. Additionally, the foyer is a passageway from the outside world into your personal refuge. A wonderful way to leave the outer world behind is to remove your shoes as you enter. This action symbolically acknowledges your home as a sanctuary. On a practical level, it helps keep the carpets and floors clean.

apartments and condominiums

If you reside in an apartment or condominium, you may have no control over the outside of the building, making it difficult to implement remedies to the main entrance. If you believe that your building could use some feng shui adjustments, ask the management for permission to incorporate them. Wind chimes and plants are usually well received, especially if you offer to buy them. In shared hallways, place a plant outside your door, a welcome mat on the ground, or a wreath of silk flowers or beautiful picture on the door. If you are not able to enhance the exterior, the foyer to your apartment becomes even more crucial. You must supply an abundance of energy directly inside if the outer hallway is dark and barren. The true first impression is established inside the door of your apartment.

ABOVE: A round-faceted crystal hangs prettily from a chandelier in this elegant foyer, while tall orchids on the table create a slight barrier for energy traveling down the staircase.

energy inside your home

Your foyer channels energy to the rest of your home. Your house needs to "marinate," in the energy that flows through the front entrance. Your goal is to have optimum energy circulating into every corner of your dwelling. If your house is unable to hold this energy, it may manifest as financial loss, ill health, or missed opportunities. The following are situations where energy leaves the home before it can circulate properly. Implement the correct solutions so that your home can support you.

Stairs at the Entrance

If your entrance opens up to a flight of stairs, energy rushes up, back down, and exits before you have closed the door (see opposite page).

Solution

- Hang a crystal ball between the door and the first step of the stairs to keep the energy circulating. It should hang at least two inches below the top of the door frame.

Door Alignment

If your entrance is directly opposite a back door, large window, or sliding glass door, energy enters and leaves much too quickly (see page 171).

Solutions

- Hang a crystal ball or wind chime halfway between the front and back door or window to keep energy in the house. The crystal and the tubes of the wind chime should hang at least two inches below the top of the front door frame.
- Place a small tree, hanging plant, or piece of furniture between the two doors to stop the energy from leaving.

Bathroom at the Entrance

If a bathroom is located by the entrance, vital energy is being flushed down the drains and toilet. Because water represents the flow of wealth, your finances and career opportunities can be washed away.

Solutions

- Keep the toilet seat down and the bathroom door closed at all times.
- Place a mirror on the outside of the door to reflect the favorable energy away from the bathroom if the bathroom is not directly opposite the main door.
- Do not use this bathroom if you can avoid it.
- Implement the suggestions for power bathrooms on page 116.

Mirror Opposite Entrance

If you face a mirror when you first enter your home, energy is being reflected back out the door before it has a chance to circulate inside. Mirrors are great feng shui in foyers but not when hung directly opposite the door. You should hang a mirror opposite your door only to deflect negative energy away from your house. This indoor mirror works the same way a convex mirror above the outside of your door works.

Solution
• Move the mirror to a sidewall to keep the foyer bright and open.

foyer design

Feng shui teaches you to create an entrance that welcomes you with love, beauty, peace, and abundant living energy. The first sight and smell you receive must be uplifting. As a homecoming ritual, you may want to light a scented candle to enhance your mood and emotions. Your home is one place you can control, so create the exact feeling you desire as you walk in the door. If your job is chaotic, hang a photo of a tranquil setting in the entryway to encourage relaxation. If you live in a metropolitan city, you may want to shift your attention to nature by placing a water fountain and plants in the foyer. If you crave excitement, become motivated with a colorful picture of racing horses and a vase of bright red and orange flowers.

As mentioned in chapter four, displaying your favorite piece of art inside your front entrance influences your state of mind. It sees you off and welcomes you home. Art in the foyer also represents your essence to a guest entering your home for the first time. It immediately reveals your passions, values, morals, and life views. As you leave the outer world behind, your inspiring piece of art reminds you of your dreams. Look back at your answers to your life questions. What do you want to manifest right now? Do you wish for serenity or passion, beauty or balance, success or self-knowledge? Do you own a piece of art or could you buy one that symbolizes your overall aspiration? Make it a powerful environmental anchor and place it across from the front door. The rule is that you must love it.

a clear passageway

You will reap the benefits of positive energy flowing into your home by keeping the foyer clean, well lit, and uncluttered. Make sure that the doorbell and doorknob function correctly and have a delightful sound. Your intention is to welcome yourself and all of your guests with love and graciousness. Energy will flow generously into your home if you correct the following unfavorable situations.

RIGHT: If an entrance opens to a direct view of the back door, your finances and vitality may be jeopardized. Suspend a crystal or wind chime in the foyer and arrange furniture, such as a side table with plants, to keep money and health from exiting though the back door.

Dark Entry

If you open your door into a dark cavelike atmosphere, vital energy dissipates immediately. In darkness, your own energy constricts and deflates causing depression, loneliness, and a lack of motivation.

Solutions

- Pull back the curtains, open the windows, and let the natural sunlight bathe your entry.
- Paint it a light color and install a ceiling light fixture with a full-spectrum bulb.
- Utilize a standing halogen lamp to lift oppressive energy towards the ceiling.

Cluttered Entry

Energy cannot move freely in a foyer overflowing with newspapers, umbrellas, shopping bags, coats, keys, mail, and shoes. Clutter immediately depletes your energy, and it is inappropriate for your guests to wade through a mess.

Solutions

- Clear clutter from the floor, dust your furniture, and return everything to its proper place within the home.
- Remove all clutter from behind the door so that it can open wide to welcome opportunities.

Confined Entry

If your foyer is small and claustrophobic, energy becomes cramped and stifled.

Solutions

- Place a large mirror on a side wall of the foyer.
- Place a plant in front of the mirror to double the lively energy.
- Hang a painting that has depth or a three-dimensional quality such as a landscape or seascape. Incorporate a scene that gives the illusion of looking out a window.
- Paint the area a light color and add a light source.

---

colors for the foyer

The foyer looks and feels the best in light and vibrant colors that welcome you. The light colors will allow the natural sunlight coming through the door to reflect off the walls to lift the energy. Avoid dark colors because they tend to constrict an area and make it feel small and dismal. However, you may paint the foyer a darker color if it is exceptionally large. If you want a dark color, incorporate a lamp and furniture in light colors to add vitality. Desirable colors for the foyer are white, off-white, beige, cream, and light shades of green, yellow, peach, and pink.

Blocked or Split Entry

If your door opens up to a wall or closet, it becomes a "brick wall," preventing energy from circulating inside. This may cause loss in finances, health, and career advancements. Another problem occurs when your door opens to a split view in which one eye focuses on the wall closest to you and the other on an extended view into another room. Two rooms split by a wall may disturb the balance of your perception, leading to confusion, nervousness, and relationship difficulties.

Solutions

• For both blocked and split entryways where a wall greets you, hang a painting that has depth or a three-dimensional quality such as a landscape or seascape. This creates the illusion of a larger, expanded view, drawing you into the house.

• In a split-view entryway, eliminate the impact of confusion by hanging three-dimensional art that focuses your attention in only one direction.

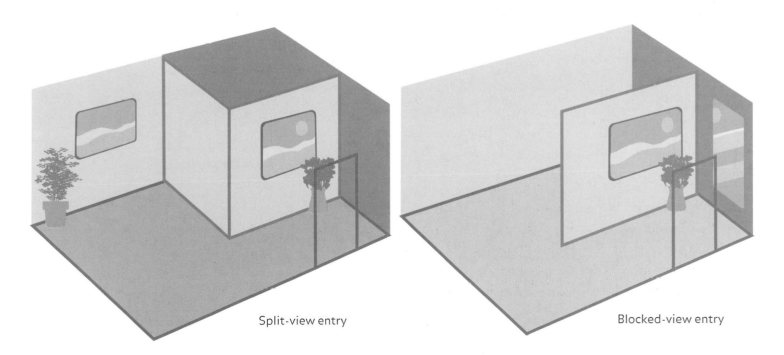

Split-view entry

Blocked-view entry

hallways

Hallways are passageways that guide energy throughout the home. They can be embellished to slow down or speed up energy depending on your particular layout. Decorating hallways with artwork, small tables with flowers or trinkets, potted plants, and mirrors adds style and good feng shui. Think of hallways as mini rooms to beautify. Enjoy your journey from one room to another by using the space to display family photos and treasured antiques. Hang art that has depth to simulate looking out of a window. Skylights add natural sunlight to a dark hallway, and wall sconces create style and artificial light.

Long hallways create fast-moving energy, which is unfavorable. Just as water rushes down a straight river, the energy charges down the hallway, bombarding whatever stands at the end of it.

If there is a bathroom at the end of the hallway, the energy (health and finances) will go straight down the toilet.

If a back door or window is at the end of a hallway, the energy will go straight outside without circulating in the home.

If your bedroom is at the end of a hallway, the force of the energy flowing may cause sleep or health problems.

If your office is at the end, it might be uncomfortable sitting at your desk and/or staying in the room for any length of time.

Solutions

Use one or more of these recommendations to slow down the energy:

• Hang a round faceted crystal or a wind chime in the middle of the hallway. Make sure that the crystal or wind chime hangs at least two inches below the top of the nearest door frame.

• Add artwork to the hallway to take the focus away from what is at the end.

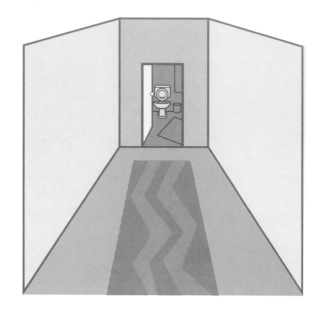

ABOVE: Quickly moving energy, along with money and health, rushes down an empty hallway and escapes down the toilet.

ABOVE: Hang a crystal and place plants and artwork in a long hallway to slow the energy down. Remember to keep the bathroom door closed.

- Place a large, heavy object such as a statue, potted plant, or small table in the hall. A narrow bookcase filled with books will further stabilize a long hallway.
- Place a rug or runner to absorb and contain the energy.

On the other hand, cluttered hallways stop energy from flowing altogether. If your hallway is filled with a lot of furniture, magazines, trash, broken items, and dirty clothes, the energy is stagnating. You must clear it so the energy has space to circulate throughout the rest of the home. Don't let it get stuck. Clogging the arteries starves the rest of your home of beneficial energy. If the hallway has been cluttered for a long time, cleanse the space by burning sandalwood incense after you have cleared it.

Solutions

Here are a few suggestions to get energy moving·
- Remove the clutter.
- Paint the hallway a light color.
- Add a light fixture or sconce to brighten it up. Crystal lamps stimulate energy.
- Hang a lively, vibrant piece of art above eye level to lift the energy up from the floor.
- Hang a mirror to open and expand the space.

staircases

The shape, location, and direction of a staircase are important factors in determining if it is encouraging or diminishing the energy of the house. The shape of the staircase determines the way the energy flows. In general, wide and gently curved staircases are the best because they allow the energy to flow smoothly, not too fast and not too slowly. Rounded banisters are highly recommended. A straight, narrow staircase can cause a direct descent, forcing the energy to fall quickly downward. Spiral staircases are problematic since the energy plummets down the center as if draining to the floor.

Staircases with landings are advantageous in allowing the energy to slow down and breathe before making the final descent. Placing a potted plant,

statue, or seat with pillows on a landing stabilizes it. If your stairs do not have risers, place small potted plants (silk or live) between each step to stop the energy from slipping through the stairs.

Solutions

To stabilize the energy of staircases, implement some of the following:

- Hang a crystal or crystal chandelier at the top of the staircase to hold the energy up high.
- Hang a crystal at the bottom of the staircase if the staircase leads down to a door. The crystal should be halfway between the base and the door at least two inches below the top of the door frame.
- Ground the energy by placing heavy objects such as planters, stones, statues, or small pieces of furniture at the base.
- Hang photographs and pictures in a stairwell to balance the energy and to make it an enjoyable walk up or down the stairs.
- Weave garlands of silk flowers or vines around banisters in steep or narrow stairwells to slow down and circulate the energy.
- Keep the staircases well lit with natural light or lighting fixtures in order to see where you are going. This adds a sense of a light at the end of the tunnel.

entrance rooms

Which room welcomes you when you step inside the front door? Typically, the foyer or living room greets you and provides a place to put down your belongings before moving into the rest of your home. However, if your door opens up into a kitchen, office, laundry room, or bedroom, your focus may go in an unintended direction. Homes that open up to the kitchen or dining room may promote weight problems. You are immediately reminded to eat every time you come home. If your eyes rest on your office, you might feel that your tasks are never completed. If your door opens up to a full view of your bedroom, you may find it difficult to motivate yourself and to get things accomplished. That cozy bed always seems to be calling your name.

Solutions

- Divert your attention from an undesired room by keeping the door closed.

LEFT: A wide, curving staircase allows energy to flow gently from one floor to another.

- Hang a curtain or place a screen or a large plant to obscure the view if the room has no door.
- Hang a large colorful piece of art to redirect your focus to another area of the home.

If your entrance is into your laundry room, you might feel as if your housework is never finished. A room full of dirty laundry, garbage, and mops and cleaners does not represent good feng shui. Your energy shouldn't drop the minute you step inside.

Solutions
- Embellish your laundry room by adding live or silk plants and flowers, colorful artwork, and curtains to hide cleaning products.
- Use a shelf to display scented candles, fresh flowers, pictures of friends and family, and other inspirational items.

the foyer and the bagua
Where is your foyer in relation to the bagua of your home? Usually, it will be in Helpful People, Career, or Knowledge and Wisdom. Since a healthy plant and a lamp energize any center, cover yourself and at least implement those enhancements. If your foyer is in Career, a water fountain will work wonders. Refer to chapter six for further tips on the bagua.

RIGHT: An uncluttered foyer with voluminous natural light, cheerful colors, and fresh flowers creates an optimal passageway for energy to pass through.

take action now

What is your foyer saying about you? How can you enhance the look, feel, and smell? Here are some practical suggestions to generate instantaneous change:

1. **Clear the clutter from behind the door.** Dust the furniture, sweep the floor, and clean the mirrors in the entry.

2. **Hang a crystal or wind chime** if you can see a back door or window from the entry. The crystal should be halfway between the two to contain the energy. If a flight of stairs greets you, hang a crystal between the stairs and the front door at least two inches below the top of the door frame.

3. **Close the door and lower the toilet seat** if a bathroom is located near the entrance. This will prevent the energy from going down the drain.

4. **Add a bright light, a healthy plant**, and a mirror to open up the space for more energy to pass through the foyer.

5. **Find your favorite piece of art** and place it in the foyer. Add beloved items such as picture frames, vases, and candles to add color and meaning to the space.

179

eight:
the bedroom
and bathroom

Use feng shui enhancements to encourage rejuvenation, serenity, and intimacy in the more private spaces of your home. A beautiful bedroom and bathroom can renew your spirit and create harmony at the start and finish of each day.

the bedroom

The bedroom is one of the rooms you relish most. Whether you are at work, school, out of town, or on daily errands, the dream of relaxing in your cozy bedroom repeats itself over and over again. The phrase, "There's no place like home," conjures up the image of sleeping in your bed, surrounded by all your creature comforts. The bedroom provides a place to rest, revitalize, and reflect as well as to communicate and encourage romance with a companion. It should be a nourishing sanctuary.

The best way to create this refuge is to surround yourself with objects you love to see, touch, taste, smell, and hear. Your senses must bathe in tranquility. In fact, the best location for a bedroom is in the back of the house, away from the commotion of cars, neighbors, and outside noise; the more relaxing it is, the better. Since connecting with yourself and your partner is a priority, a supportive environment that assures well-being, comfort, and privacy is optimal. For sound sleep, keep only a minimal number of books near your bedside. Remove computers, work projects, and bills (especially unpaid ones). If there is absolutely no other place for these items, place them in a drawer or cover them with a scarf or piece of fabric after dealing with them.

Bedroom décor should be soft, warm, inviting, and graceful. Decorate with your favorite colors and fabrics. Soft pillows, flowing drapes, handmade quilts, and silky bedding enhance serenity because fabric calms the energy. Beneficial fabrics include silks, satins, cottons, flannels, and velvets. For texture, you can also weave in floral prints, pastel stripes, gingham, sheers, damask, and lace. To bring in color, accent the room with rugs, linens, pottery, art, and picture frames. Furniture made from natural materials works well in the bedroom. Wood such as pine, oak, teak, and rattan deliver the earth's energy. A chaise lounge, love seat, or overstuffed chair provides a great place to read, write, or cuddle.

PREVIOUS PAGE: An overstuffed, floral-print comforter, cozy pillows, and antique screen-turned-headboard create the setting for a heavenly night's sleep. Wake feeling refreshed with ample sunlight and fresh flowers.

colors for the bedroom

Soft and soothing colors belong in the bedroom. If you prefer warmer colors, stick to the creams, peaches, pinks, peaches, and earth tones. If you prefer cooler colors, go with light greens, blues, and lavender. Blues calm; pinks and peaches invite love and romance; accents of red, pomegranate, and burgundy bring excitement and passion.

your bed

Jumping into bed at night is blissful. It is amazing to realize that most people spend one-third of their lives in bed. It is the spot where some of the most special, profound, and intimate moments take place. Consider the activities that occur in bed. You sleep, read, play, relax, write, dream, connect with your partner, and become inspired for the day ahead. Creating a calm, gentle, and warm energy around your bed will help you sleep more soundly and allow you to awaken feeling renewed and revitalized.

A good night's sleep is essential in order to be physically healthy, emotionally strong, and spiritually sound. Sleep influences your performance, mental focus, productivity, and coping skills throughout the entire day. Be sure to clear clutter from under your bed. You must keep that space empty and clean, so energy can circulate freely while you sleep. If you are one of those people who store work papers, bills, or files under the bed, stop doing that. Your sleep will be more restful because work and finances will not plague you during the night. Store your vocational items in filing cabinets.

ABOVE: A wooden headboard offers protection and grounding; its rounded edges and the nightstand's circular shape contribute to a healthy rest.

The headboard represents stability and support. It creates a firm backing and protection to your head as you sleep. Solid wood headboards are the best since they are heavy and bring in the energy of trees. If you have a metal or wrought-iron headboard or one with open slats, you can weave silk ribbon, garlands or faux vines, or some other attractive trim around the slats to soften and warm the energy. Silk protects your energy from leaking out, allowing you to awaken feeling strong and vibrant. Canopy beds should have rounded dowels and no sharp edges. If your bed has square dowels, soften them with fabric, silk vines, or garlands.

the mighty mattress

Every night, you spend six to nine hours on top of your mattress. On a physical level, the mattress cushions, comforts, and supports your body during slumber. On an energy level, it holds your thoughts, emotions, stress, arguments, and illnesses. Since many activities occur in bed, various kinds of energy build up over time. When you experience stress or arguments in bed, the energy expressed in those disturbing moments lingers inside the mattress.

I recommend that you buy a new mattress every seven or eight years or after any significant illness or relationship. When you lie in bed with an illness, the disease and upset seep into the mattress. If you shared a bed with a former companion, the energy of your relationship still exists within the mattress. It becomes saturated with unwanted energy that continually surrounds you. To bring in vibrant health or a new love, make sure to change your mattress. Additionally, although water is good feng shui, waterbeds are not. Water, which absorbs energy even faster than a normal mattress, exacerbates the past energy issue.

If you cannot buy a new mattress, implement these solutions to cleanse an old one:

- Place the mattress outside in direct sunlight for at least eight hours. Wave sandalwood incense around it before bringing it back inside.
- Perform a salt burning in the bedroom (see page 83) after an illness, break up, or divorce.

proper feng shui for the bed

The proper placement for your bed offers you strength and protection. Locating the bed in the correct area of the room will improve your overall health. The best position for the bed is in the back corner of the room, diagonally opposite the door. This site provides grounding and power because of the solid wall behind the bed, the expanded view of the room and door, and protection from fast-moving energy entering the space. Placing the bed on a diagonal in the back corner is also fine, but make sure you have a solid headboard to protect your head. A lamp that shines light toward the ceiling or a silk plant in the corner behind the bed works to fill the empty space. If possible, try placing your bed so that your head points

a tidy bed

The simple act of making your bed every morning will help you start the day in an organized fashion. Pulling up the covers and arranging your pillows will allow your day to begin with wonderful self-care. Magically, once the bed is made, the room looks and feels clean. It takes two or three minutes, and the reward is a beautiful bedroom that beckons you at the end of the day.

RIGHT: The calming, neutral-colored bedding is accented by a splash of red, encouraging passion in the bedroom. A new mattress ensures healthy energy flow while eliminating the negative impact of past illnesses, bad relationships, or distress.

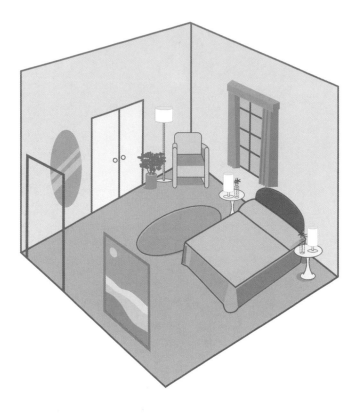

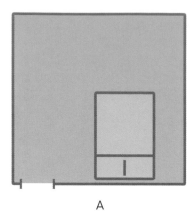

A

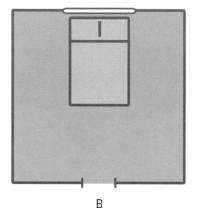

B

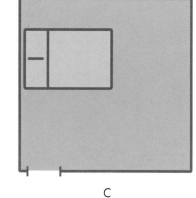

C

east when you lie down. The eastern energy is associated with the rising sun and with spiritual energies that bring health and harmony. The following are bed positions to avoid and some feng shui fixes for them:

Bed next to the Door

A bed next to the door does not allow you to easily view the door and potential visitors (see right, A).

Solutions

- Place a small mirror on the opposite wall to view the door from your bed.
- Do not allow a mirror to reflect the bed.

Bed on a Direct Line with the Door

A bed that is on a direct line with the door allows energy bustling down the hall to strike you, disturbing your sleep. Additionally, it may cause your personal energy to drain out the door (see right, B and C).

ABOVE: The above left illustration shows excellent bed, window, art, and mirror placement for the bedroom. Illustrations A, B, and C show bed positions that should be avoided if possible.

ABOVE: Sleeping in a bed that's backed by a wall and is near a window with a pleasing view to outdoors keeps you fortified and energized throughout the day.

Solutions

- Close the door at night.
- Make a "door" by hanging silk curtains or placing a screen between your bed and the door.
- Create a barrier between you and the door with a footboard that is at least one foot above the mattress. A small table or trunk at the foot of your bed works, too.
- Hang a round crystal halfway between the bed and the door, two inches below the door frame to disperse higher energies.

windows

Like the front door, windows allow positive energy to come into the home. Maintaining clean windows gives you clarity in viewing the outside world. Dirty windows are similar to smudged eyeglasses: your vision becomes distorted. When you wake up in the morning, you should behold the true brilliance of blue sky and green trees. Follow these recommendations for good "window" feng shui in the bedroom.

- If your bed is under the window, excessive energy may be flowing in and out above your head as you sleep, causing insomnia or other sleep problems. Move the bed to a solid wall or hang silk curtains over the window and close at night. You can also install wooden shutters (see page 186 B).
- If large windows or doors are opposite the bed, your energy may be draining out the window during the night. To protect your energy, create a barrier such as a footboard or small piece of furniture between you and the window and hang silk curtains that you can close at night.
- If a bedroom window looks out onto a long straight road, the forceful energy from cars coming towards you can disrupt the peaceful energy of the room. Move your bedroom to a different room or place a convex mirror on the outside of the window to push back the energy. Place plants outside the window to further disperse negative energy.
- If you have an unpleasant neighbor or unsightly view, place a convex mirror on the outside of the window to deflect the negative energy.

the healthy bedroom

Health is one of the focal points in the bedroom. In order to regenerate and revitalize during sleeping hours, you must surround yourself with only positive energy. What exactly does that mean? In feng shui terms, the energy emitted from certain objects and structural elements can cause irritation or ill health if not remedied. Below you will find recommendations for mirrors, exposed beams, sharp corners, slanted ceilings, and electronic equipment as they relate to the bedroom.

Mirrors

Mirrors are too stimulating for the bedroom. Energy should be calm and relaxing to promote sound sleep. Mirrors speed up and energize a space; therefore, you should not have multiple mirrors in the bedroom. In addition, a feng shui rule states that you should never see yourself in a mirror as you lay in bed, given that a mirror multiplies what it reflects. If a mirror watches you when you are sick, depressed, or stressed, it will magnify that energy. It will also amplify upsetting dreams. However, you have several choices of how to remedy mirrored closets, vanities, and armoires that stare at you during the night.

Solutions

- Do not place a mirror directly opposite the bedroom door because it will push beneficial energy back out of the room and prevent correct circulation.
- Cover all mirrors facing you in bed with a scarf or fabric before going to sleep.
- Hide mirrored closets with curtains, fabric, or wallpaper. You can also replace the mirrored closets with wooden doors. For a quick fix, before going to bed, simply open the closet door that is reflecting the majority of your upper body.
- Place the mirror inside a closet and close the closet door at night.
- Move the mirror to a side wall to generate more light or to make a bedroom appear larger. The mirror should not reflect you, the door, or a window.

Beams

Exposed beams exert downward pressure. Low-hanging beams create oppressive energy that can cause health problems, especially when they are positioned above your bed. The beams send energy downward on specific parts of the body while you sleep. When this occurs every night for many years, it can manifest negatively on those areas of the body. Additionally, relationship difficulties can arise if a beam cuts down the middle of the bed, separating you from your partner. If at all feasible, move your bed from beneath any exposed beams. If that is impossible, use the following solutions.

Solutions
- Paint the beams the same color as the ceiling to minimize the effect.
- Hang two or three crystals or small wind chimes underneath the beam to disperse energy. You can stagger your chosen enhancements at equal lengths along the beam.
- Hide the beams by hanging silk fabric or a canopy over them to insulate the energy (see Illustration A).
- Wrap silk flowers or vines around beams to soften the downward pressure.

Slanted Ceilings
In the same vein, slanted ceilings cause energy to slide downward. For this reason, do not place your bed underneath a slanted ceiling. The energy may be falling down on you, causing headaches or other health problems.

Solutions
- Hang a silk canopy over the bed to hide the slant.
- Hang a crystal on the slant to hold the energy up.

Sharp and Protruding Corners on Furniture
Furniture with sharp corners such as square night tables, chests, bureaus, and headboards are health concerns in feng shui. If a sharp corner is pointing at you while you sleep for six to nine hours a night, it creates a laser beam of energy that pierces you. These laser beams can cause health problems in the area they are pointing. All furniture should have rounded edges (see Illustration B).

BELOW: A good solution for exposed beams is to hang a canopy as shown in Illustration A. In addition, a plant placed in front of a protruding wall disperses sharp energy shooting towards the bed. Illustration B shows the negative effects of pointed corners on nightstands, walls, and beams.

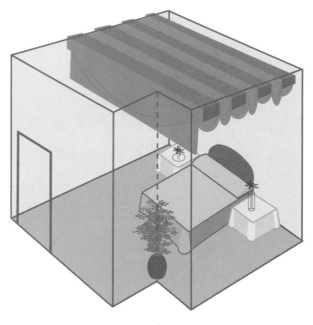

A

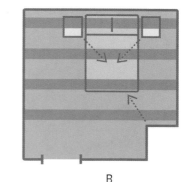

B

closets of joy

Clearing clutter to create a neatly arranged closet will promote peace, productivity, and happiness when you leave the house. In order to feel confident and good about yourself as you begin the day, keep only the clothes that you love and that fit you in your main closet. Separate your clothes by color and choose the ones that will uplift you or relax you throughout the day. When possible, treat yourself to dry cleaning and a laundry service. Clothes that are clean, pressed, and ready to wear make getting dressed a pleasure. Don't spend every Saturday doing laundry; free yourself to live out your passions. Pick up shoes, belts, trash, and mishmash from the floor to raise the energy off the ground. Dust the shelves, sweep the floor, and vacuum the carpet. Add sufficient light so you can see what you have to wear. Hang a wind chime from the ceiling of all closets to circulate the energy. Remember, in feng shui, closets count.

Solutions

- Drape silk fabric, silk vines or flowers, or a live plant over the pointed edge to soften it and to disperse the energy.
- Stick putty over extremely sharp points or edges and then cover them.

Sharp and Protruding Corners of Walls

You must also be aware of the sharp corners coming from walls that protrude into a room. These walls exude the same kind of piercing energy as furniture and also need to be dispersed.

Solutions

- Place a bushy plant in front of the corner for a softening effect.
- Hang a crystal in front of the corner.
- Avoid placing your bed near this type of corner.

electronic equipment in the bedroom

Computers, treadmills, and other electronic exercise equipment, stereos, VCRs, and televisions radiate electromagnetic energy that is detrimental to health, fertility, and serene sleep. For good feng shui, avoid placing electronics in the bedroom. If you must have a piece of electronic equipment in the room, place a plant next to it and drape it with silk fabric when you're not using it. Electric blankets are not desirable for the same reasons.

If at all possible, remove the television from the bedroom as well. At night, television programs are usually violent, controversial, and disturbing, especially the news. If you fall asleep in front of the television, your subconscious is being programmed by shows that you are not necessarily choosing to watch. Invite introspection by reading an inspiring book, writing in a journal, or connecting with a loved one before sleep. Concentrate on encouraging happy dreams and a restful repose.

On the other hand, if you wish to have a television in the bedroom, keep it inside a cabinet or covered with a scarf. Make sure you turn it off before bed and close the cabinet. As far as energy is concerned, it performs in the same way as a mirror does. You should not be able to see yourself in the television.

a serene bedroom

Once you have created a healthy bedroom, you can add plants, flowers, and light to harmonize the environment. Plants in the corners of the room lift the energy and enhance the bagua. If you'd like, place one in the back left for money and the back right for love. Colorful live or silk flowers circulate energy and beauty. Avoid live plants behind your head because they emit carbon dioxide at night.

Let sunlight bathe your room. The natural light revitalizes your body and spirit upon waking. At night, you can create warm and muted indirect

LEFT: Fresh flowers offer color and vibrant energy in this guest room. Its cool palette and sunlight combine for a light, airy feel.

lighting. Install dimmer switches to control the amount of light you desire and conserve electricity. The dimming effect is wonderful for contemplation, romantic interludes, or just relaxing. If your bedroom is particularly dark, use standing lamps in the corners to cast light towards the ceiling. Additionally, place round lampshades on all overhead lights to soften the downward pressure of the beam. A pair of wall sconces with pastel-colored light bulbs can add warmth to the environment.

Do not hang ceiling fans directly above where your upper body rests while you are in bed. Instead, hang them closer to the foot of your bed. In this position, they will not interfere with your personal energy field during sleep. In general, fans are good feng shui, especially during the day when they help circulate energy. You can attach a round, faceted crystal to the bottom of the pull chains to disperse the energy further.

ABOVE: Plants, lamps, and lively accent colors uplift your energy. Soft area rugs provide cushion and warmth all year round.

Candlelight and aroma enhance your mood in a variety of ways. Colorful candles bring harmony and romance while scented pillows, aromatherapy candles, and perfumed lining paper infuse fragrance into the bedroom. Remember to avoid potpourri. They are dried flowers and, therefore, are not recommended. Try using a diffuser with essential oils. Ylang-ylang, jasmine, rose, geranium, and sandalwood oils incite passion and love.

inspiring artwork

The first and last impression of the day powerfully influences your psyche. These images are engraved on your subconscious and send messages to you throughout the day and night. When you set your eyes on an image or object you adore, you immediately instill positive energy into your spirit. A painting portraying a lush landscape, tranquil seascape, or your favorite vacation spot should hang directly across from your bed.

In fact, any piece of art that motivates you to begin your day with a smile is worth its weight in gold. Love, abundance, and color should be prominent. Personal photographs that transport you to a place of beauty or remind you of a wonderful time in your life are other options. Since opportunities are waiting to flow into your lap, the bedroom is the perfect spot to hang a manifestation board displaying your wishes for love, creativity, success, and health. Place the board in your closet if you prefer privacy. Make sure the symbolism in your bedroom evokes positive images and memories. Clear away objects from past relationships or any item that represents a negative thought or situation. Above your bed, you can hang beautiful tapestries, colorful fabrics, or rugs. Avoid jagged, angular, or geometric patterns that might disrupt your sleep.

ABOVE: A bouquet of pink and red roses is a fitting enhancement to heat up love and passion in the bedroom.

RIGHT: An intertwining loveseat summons intimacy and stabilizes this regal canopy bed. Rounded dowels and flowing fabric soften the frame, also providing desired privacy.

new love

The bedroom is a perfect and fitting place to manifest a new relationship. Begin by energizing the Love and Relationships center in the right corner of the room (see pages 127-129). Here are more recommendations to create a sensual bedroom that stirs your heart:

- Spark momentum by hanging a round, faceted crystal from the ceiling in the Love corner.
- Arrange objects in pairs: two lamps, two candles, two picture frames, or two small plants to create the aura of a couple. A nightstand on each side of your bed symbolizes an invitation for a new companion.
- Use colors that open your heart such as pinks, whites, peaches, and reds.
- Drape a burgundy blanket on the bed.
- Sleep on peach sheets to entice a new admirer.
- Stimulate love by placing a statue of a couple in an embrace and other art that embodies passion, playfulness, and tenderness.
- Add one delightful element for each of your five senses. Play soft music, touch silky bedding, sip your favorite wine, and see and smell a bouquet of roses.

the master bedroom

Your bedroom can possess the energy of a beautiful, romantic getaway. I encourage my clients to fashion their bedroom after a favorite hotel suite. Of course, you want to add your own personal touch and mementos. Your goal is to create a sanctuary where you can leave the world, family, careers and stress behind, if only for a few hours. Simply moving around ten items will transform the space, especially if the furniture has remained in the same configuration for many years.

A loveseat, instead of chairs, invites intimacy. Find one on which you both fit comfortably with your arms and legs slightly overlapping. Buy new pillows for the bed in colors of crimson, pomegranate, eggplant, and magenta to spice up your relationship. A picture from your wedding or honeymoon and a vase of flowers will energize the Love and Relationships center. Be sure to update old pictures. Remove ones that remind you of unhappy times. Recent photos of the two of you on a fantastic vacation or special occasion are perfect for the night tables. Since your bedroom is a haven for you and your companion, you should relocate pictures of your children and parents to another room. The "fire of love" could be snuffed out if your focus turns to them in an intimate moment. Dedicate your bedroom to love, connection, and blissful sleep

ABOVE: Promote sound sleep by positioning the bed against a wall with a view of the door. Pastel colors calm a child after a stimulating school day.

LEFT: Sunlight and rounded green furniture bring healing energy into this room. The fish attract good fortune, and a lamp illuminates the corner at night.

colors for a child's bedroom

The best colors to use in a child's room are light pastels such as green, blue, beige, pink, peach, lavender, cream, and tan. To soothe an overly stimulated child, add medium shades of blue. To motivate a quiet child, add a few accents in bright colors such as yellow, red, and orange.

your child's rooms

Applying the principles of feng shui in your child's rooms can enhance imagination, learning ability, and confidence. In most cases, your child uses the bedroom for sleeping, studying, and playing. Consequently, the room accumulates clutter very quickly. The excess creates unnecessary stimulation making it difficult for a child to sleep and to concentrate on homework. You must clear the room, closets, and bureaus of outgrown and unwanted clutter. Help your child decide which clothes, books, toys, and stuffed animals to give away or store. Explain that cleaning out the old stuff makes room for new things.

The bed positions for a child's room are the same as discussed earlier. Make sure the room has ample sunlight or uses full-spectrum bulbs. The corners should be well lit to avoid dark areas. To fix an oppressive low ceiling, paint it light blue with white billowy clouds to imitate the sky. This image will encourage your child to dream and be imaginative. If the room is too small, clear out large pieces of furniture such as armoires, bookcases, and desks because they create stagnant energy.

Take down items that are hanging above your child's head. An abundance of mobiles, flying animals, and overflowing shelves create fear. Your child feels more secure when he is not concerned about items falling on his head at night. Build shelving in chests, closets, and bookcases to organize your child's daily belongings. Use a round bin or hamper to store stuffed animals and toys.

Your Child's Goals

You must create a bedroom that advances at the same rate as your child. Be mindful of the delicate balance between security objects such as stuffed animals and newer items that symbolize your child's present and future life. Display school and extra-curricular accomplishments such as band, drama, and sports awards to give the child a sense of pride and self-esteem. At the end of the school year, sift through art projects and store their favorites in a portfolio. The best situation is when a child has a separate space for schoolwork. Your child will sleep more soundly if the constant stress of homework assignments is not surrounding him. If you prefer to keep the desk in the room, cover the computer and work materials with a piece of fabric when they are not in use.

Help your child to achieve her goals by making a manifestation board. In high school, you can encourage your child to put up pictures of the college she wants to attend as well as of career goals. Sponsor a collage-making party with her friends. Remove violent, depressing, or sexual imagery and artwork from the room. Stimulate her manifesting potential with positive reinforcement.

the bathroom

The bathroom is the space dedicated to cleansing and purifying the body. Soaking and unwinding in the bathtub, steaming and lathering in the shower, or simply splashing your face with water restores health and refreshes your emotions. The very presence of water renews your spirit. Additionally, water represents prosperity in feng shui. While an abundance of water increases wealth, water that flows away from the home is not advantageous. Applying feng shui principles to your bathroom provides you with an opportunity to increase your health and wealth.

The bathroom can cause problems because water is escaping down the drains and the toilet every day. In chapter five, you discovered where each bathroom was located in terms of the nine energy centers and the many ways to enhance them. Nonetheless, in order to create excellent feng shui bathrooms, a few more solutions and enhancements are vital. You can enjoy the bathing experience and create positive energy simultaneously.

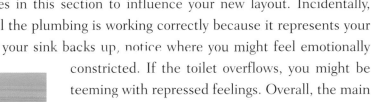

BELOW: A vivacious green bathroom emits healing vibrations while multiple mirrors and light fixtures activate and uplift energy.

Location is everything. If you are planning to remodel or build a home, use the guidelines in this section to influence your new layout. Incidentally, make sure all the plumbing is working correctly because it represents your emotions. If your sink backs up, notice where you might feel emotionally constricted. If the toilet overflows, you might be teeming with repressed feelings. Overall, the main goal is to strengthen the energy in the bathroom while separating it from the rest of the home. Transform it into a place of power and beauty by stopping the drain and energizing with gusto.

bathroom energy

You will find many ways to uplift the energy in your bathroom. To begin, you need to fully comprehend the toilet issue. As far as the drains go, the toilet is the most detrimental since it possesses the largest opening. In addition, the flushing mechanism creates a strong suction that pulls the energy downward and out of your home. Keeping the bathroom door closed and toilet seat down minimizes the loss of energy and money.

To further counteract the draining effect, the toilet should be as inconspicuous as possible. In fact, the best solution is to have a separate room with it's own door for the toilet only. If the toilet is in the same room as your sink and shower, position it as far away from the bathroom door as possible. In essence, you want to make it difficult for energy to find the toilet. If you have enough space, hide the toilet with a partition such as a small wall or a chest with a plant on top. Hanging silk or beaded curtains is another option. Mirrors are highly recommended for the bathroom as they speed up and circulate energy. However, to avoid multiplying the dirty energy, make sure that a large mirror is not reflecting the toilet. In other words, you shouldn't see your entire body as you are sitting on the toilet.

To energize the bathroom, invite sunlight and fresh air in with windows and skylights. The fresh air helps to dry out the bathroom, which tends to become damp and musty. If you do not have a window, open the bathroom door for a few minutes after a shower to air it out. Make sure the toilet seat is down. If the room has no window, place lamps with full-spectrum bulbs in the corners to simulate natural sunlight and to stimulate the energy.

You can strengthen the overall energy of each bathroom by implementing the correct enhancements (see page 116). At the very least, add a night-light, one to two healthy plants, and rubber stoppers to cover your drains when they are not in use. Keep the night-light on twenty-four hours a day and place the plants higher than the toilet. To raise the energy exponentially, place a tabletop water fountain on the sink or shelf allowing it to run continually. Do not place a water fountain on top of the toilet. The exception to placing a fountain in the bathroom is if it is located in the Fame and Reputation center.

great bathroom solutions

According to the principles of feng shui, the placement of each bathroom can deplete various areas of your life. Fortunately, you can use numerous solutions to remedy the bathroom dilemmas. Listed below are bathroom locations that require your swift attention.

ABOVE: Keep the toilet seat down and conceal the toilet behind a small wall or in a separate room to prevent energy and wealth from escaping down the drain. A healthy plant positioned higher than the toilet adds energy to the bathroom.

Bathroom at Entrance

If a bathroom is close to your front door, the beneficial energy will rapidly go down the drain, taking your finances, health, and good fortune with it. Outside energy will not have the opportunity to circulate throughout the home; it will head straight for the toilet. The same solution applies to a bathroom located above the front door on the second story.

Solutions

- Keep the door closed.
- Place a small convex mirror on the outside of bathroom door, and implement all of the enhancements on page 116.

Bathroom at Center of Home

If a bathroom is located in the center of your home, health issues relating to the body, mind, and spirit might be prevalent. If you have many other bathrooms, you might consider energizing this bathroom but not using it. Another alternative if you own your home, is to remove the plumbing and remodel the room into a new space. The center of your home is very special. It should be overflowing with positive energy.

Solutions

- Keep the door closed if you must use the center bathroom.
- Place a small convex mirror on the outside of bathroom door and implement all the enhancements on page 116.

Bathroom in Bedroom

Although convenient, having a bathroom in the bedroom is not a good idea. The toilet energy may be contaminating you, draining your energy while you sleep, and causing health problems. You may awake feeling exhausted.

Solutions

- Keep the bathroom door closed at all times.
- Hang a small mirror on the outside of the bathroom door. Make sure your image is not reflected in the mirror when you are in bed.
- Create a door by hanging a silk curtain, screen, or beaded curtain if there is no bathroom door. Silk will insulate the bathroom energy and keep it from draining your energy at night.
- Use all of the recommended enhancements on page 116.

the bathroom and your pets

Some people need to keep the bathroom door open to allow a pet to drink, eat, or use the litter box. The best solution is to install a small pet door for your animal. The pet will be able to enter, but large amounts of energy will not. If you live in an apartment or are unable to install a pet door, an alternate solution is to hang a silk curtain on the outside of the open door. Your animal can pass underneath, but the silk provides protection. The positive energy will stay in your home without draining out of the bathroom.

Shared Bathroom and Bedroom Wall

If a bathroom is on the other side of your bedroom wall, make sure that the toilet is not sharing the same wall as your head. The toilet contains dirty energy, and you do not want this energy pouring into you as you sleep (see right).

Solutions

- Hang silk behind your headboard to stop the energy from contaminating you if there is no other place for your bed.
- Place a convex mirror in the bathroom behind the toilet. Make sure the reflective side faces into the bathroom to deflect the toilet's energy.

Bathroom at End of Hallway

As you know, long hallways create fast-moving energy. If a bathroom is at the end of a hallway, the energy will rapidly descend down the drain causing health and wealth problems.

Solutions

- Keep the door closed.
- Place a small mirror on the outside of the bathroom door.
- Add a large, heavy item in the hallway to slow down the energy.
- Hang a round crystal in the middle of hallway at least two inches below the top of the bathroom door frame to disperse energy.
- Implement all the enhancements on page 116

Bathroom near the Stove and Desk

If your stove shares a wall with a toilet or if a toilet is located above the stove on the second floor, the dirty energy will be contaminating the food you cook. You do not want to mix kitchen energy with toilet energy. In the same way, your desk should not share a wall with a toilet, or your work and finances might suffer. Again, you want to separate the positive energy from the toilet energy.

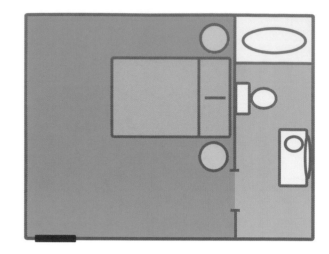

ABOVE: It is not advisable for the bed and toilet to share a wall.

a new home

If you are planning to move or build a home, pay special attention to where the bathrooms are placed. Try not to rent, buy, or build a home with bathrooms at the entrance, in the center, in the back left (Wealth and Prosperity), back right (Love and Relationships) or front middle (Career). Where should the bathrooms ideally be located? Bathrooms in the front left (Knowledge and Wisdom), middle left (Family), middle right (Creativity) and front right (Helpful People) are not as detrimental to core issues of health, wealth, and love. Don't be upset if you have found the perfect house with one poorly placed bathroom. You can boost the energy by implementing the enhancements.

Solutions

- Place a convex mirror behind the toilet with the reflective side facing into the bathroom. This will contain the toilet energy inside the bathroom by reflecting the toilet energy back into the bathroom.
- Place a convex mirror on the ceiling above the stove with the reflective side facing the ceiling if a bathroom is located above the stove. This looks a bit weird, but it does a good job of reflecting the toilet energy back upstairs.
- Move the desk to protect it.
- Place a convex mirror on the back of the desk with the reflective side facing the wall to keep the toilet energy away.

beauty in the bathroom

You will look forward to your washing and bathing experience if you add color, texture, and fragrance to the bathroom. Give it the love and adornment it deserves. For example, a decorative mirror pleases the eye. It enhances morning activities such as washing your face, shaving, combing your hair, brushing your teeth, and putting on makeup. Gluing seashells or colored stones to a mirror injects color and nature energy; draping garlands of silk flowers and vines around it will soften the edges. Make sure the mirror is not warped or broken. You want to be able to see yourself clearly. In addition, you can install wall sconces on both sides of the mirror for accent lights. For relaxation, paint the ceiling your favorite color and dim the lights while soaking in the tub. Pour a pound or two of salt in the tub to cleanse away daily stress (see page 28).

Create a home spa with fragrant aroma and visual beauty. To adorn the walls, hang a tranquil picture such as a landscape or seascape with depth. A picture will open up the space, making it feel larger. A less expensive idea is to frame an inspiring quote or greeting card and hang it on the wall. Add colored soaps, fresh or silk plants and flowers, see-through bottles of bubble bath and oils, scented candles, and incense to uplift the energy.

BELOW: Hang mirrors with ample reflective space and keep them sparkling. A seashell mirror pleases the eye and delivers nature's restorative energy.

take action now

1. **Locate your bathrooms** and decide which ones need the most energy. Can you see a correlation between the bathroom positions and your good fortune?

2. **Place a mirror** on the outside of the bathroom door if it is located in a precarious position.

3. **Post notes** in the bathroom reminding everyone to close the door and put the toilet lid down.

4. **Place a plant and night**-light inside each bathroom.

5. **Add colorful décor** and fragrant aroma to delight your senses.

6. **Take a relaxing salt bath**, light incense, and sip your favorite tea in your newly energized space.

posting notes

Change your thoughts and behaviors by posting positive reminders in visible areas of your home. Bathrooms are a great room to place notes prompting you to use mental feng shui. Daily affirmations can be placed on the wall, door, or mirror. For instance, if you are trying to stop rushing in your daily routine, stick a note on your bathroom mirror that says, "I always get ready in a relaxed way." This may seem simplistic, but seeing the new words in front of you every day really works by shifting your thinking. You must train your mind to avoid your habitual, negative words and phrases and replace them with positive, empowering ones. "Breathe and smile" is one of my favorites.

Harmonize the yin (feminine) and yang (masculine) aspects of your bathroom. Hard shiny surfaces including marble, slate, tile, granite, chrome, and glass are very yang and tend to stimulate the energy. You can balance the coolness of these heavy, slick surfaces with yin elements such as colorful, plush bath mats, towels, fabric shower curtains, and window treatments. If you have a glass shower stall, you might want to hang a fabric curtain in front of the door to soften the energy. It will add color and movement to a square, metal shower area. Wooden floors, a wooden toilet seat, stones, and pebbles are wonderful for creating a natural setting. Ultimately, you want to create a soothing and pleasurable room that invites you to rejuvenate your body and mind in purity.

ABOVE: Beautify the bathroom with your favorite paintings or prints, lamps, and other objects.

LEFT: Indulge your senses by taking a bath with essential oils, surrounded by aromatic candles, fresh air, and white orchids.

nine:

kitchen, dining, and living areas

A sense of community arises when people come together to eat, talk, and enjoy one another's company. Increasing positive energy in the kitchen, dining, and living areas optimizes happy, healthy interaction, and generates household prosperity. Putting feng shui to work in these rooms enlivens you and your environment.

the kitchen

The magical presence of food brings people together for nourishment, connection, and celebration. For many families, the kitchen is the heart of the home. Gathering morning and evening to share the events of the day and to plan the day to come creates a special environment in the kitchen. Creating a space that is bright, clean, and cheery influences the energy of the food as you prepare it and eat it. You achieve good feng shui when the kitchen and its adjoining rooms glow with a loving and positive vibration.

Cooking is a wonderfully creative outlet. The energy and love poured into homemade food sustains and heals us. Every family member, from youngest to oldest, can help to prepare a meal. Reading the recipe, assembling the ingredients, and cooking each dish create an atmosphere of communication, laughter, and a common bond. Food holds a magnetic attraction, which makes the kitchen the center of activity at family gatherings and parties.

In feng shui, the stove holds the energy for prosperity and abundance. From the beginning of time many cultures have used food as an indicator of wealth and generosity. The amount of food a person lavished upon his family and friends was a measurement of his success. Accordingly, the stove, which facilitates the feasting process, contains prosperity energy. This energy encircles the stove and overflows into the entire kitchen.

You must keep your stove clean and ensure that all burners are working correctly. The fire energy emanating from the stove stokes your home's financial abundance. Since the kitchen combines the fire and water elements represented by the stove and sink, you need to keep them separate. If a sink is located directly across or next to the stove, the water will extinguish the fire, which is not a desirable circumstance. Correct placement of these two elements will stimulate abundance for everyone living in the home.

a prosperous stove

The position of the stove is a major factor in securing affluence. You should face into the kitchen and towards the door

PREVIOUS PAGE: Harmonious energy circulates throughout a kitchen and dining area bounteous with wholesome food and lush, flowering plants.

colors for the kitchen

The best colors for the kitchen are those that support your health and nutrition. Use yellow to symbolize sunshine, green for healing, blue to calm, and white or cream for a clean palette. Terra-cotta and rich browns will ground the space. Use dark or bright colors such as red, orange, and black as accents.

as you prepare meals on the stove. Installing a stove in a center island provides ample space and places you in the power position. If your back is to the kitchen when you cook, place a small mirror above you to heighten your awareness of what is going on behind you.

As stated previously, the stove (representing fire) should not be opposite or next to the sink (representing water) or your finances could be negatively affected. To repel the water energy, place a small convex mirror on the front or side of the stove with the reflective side pointing towards the sink. On the other hand, if the stove is located in the center of your home, there may be too much fire energy, creating instability between people living in the home. In this case, add a water element to the stove to subdue the fire. A vase with fresh flowers or a teapot or glass bowl filled with water is sufficient, provided you change the water once or twice a week. If the refrigerator is next to the stove, place a convex mirror on the side of the stove to deflect the cold energy. A plant placed between them will further harmonize the two energies.

To apply feng shui principles to your stove, consider the following information and implement the enhancements:

- Remove vessels filled with water such as teapots or saucepans from the stove when they are not being used.
- Place mirrors on walls or objects on the side of your stove to reflect the burners. The burners of your stove represent money, and the mirrors will symbolically double your money. Make sure that the stove is working properly and that all burners ignite. Rotate the use of all burners throughout the week.
- Hang a wind chime over your head as you stand at the stove to call in prosperity energy. The wind chime can be small with metal tubes. It should hang a few inches from the ceiling.
- Remove all knives from the top of the stove and from the area next to it. Sharp objects should not point towards the stove since they project negative energy.
- To create loving energy, burn a stick of rose incense on the stove daily.

tips for a healthy kitchen

A sunny kitchen filled with flora encourages happy and healthy energy to permeate the space. You can place plants in the room's corners, on top of the refrigerator, and between the stove and sink to add harmony and healing to the eating area. Microwaves are not recommended. They emit electromagnetic fields and kill the nutrients in many foods. If you own one, place a plant near it to counteract some of these harmful effects.

To energize the kitchen, display fresh flowers in colorful vases for fragrant aroma and beauty. The kitchen should have an abundance of natural sunlight and fresh air; a garden window will provide more light and space for plants. In small or dark spaces, install lamps that scatter light up towards the ceiling, especially in the corners. You can also hang lights inside glass cabinets to illuminate china and stemware. In general, large mirrors are advantageous when placed in the kitchen. They increase the light, open up the room, and double the fortunate energy of the food and stove. Mirrors expand and multiply all joyous occasions.

The sink and the refrigerator are the water elements in the kitchen. As is true in the bathroom, you should keep the sink drains closed or covered with stoppers when not in use. To keep the energy level high, hang a round crystal above each drain, approximately four inches from the ceiling. The crystal helps to prevent energy and, symbolically, money from escaping down the drain. Make sure the countertops are clean and cleared of clutter including spices, appliances, bills, containers, and condiments. These impede calm cooking conditions.

Wood butcher blocks work well in the kitchen, bringing in nature energy and warming the space; granite and tile countertops speed up energy, so you can add plants to calm and harmonize. Make sure all the countertops have rounded edges to diminish "sharp" energy coming at you while you are cooking. You can add live or silk plants to soften a sharp corner if necessary. To encourage participation and communication, place bar stools underneath the counter.

LEFT: Natural light and energy stream in a garden window illuminating plants, flowers, and charming kitchen décor.

The floor should be comfortable and gentle on your feet and legs. Natural wooden floors are best because you tend to stand in the kitchen for long periods of time. Slate, limestone, ceramic tile, and marble offer a sleek look, but they are very cold in the winter. A colorful rug on the kitchen floor provides warmth and cushioning.

an organized kitchen

An orderly kitchen promotes successful, enjoyable cooking. Knowing the exact location of each ingredient and kitchen accessory is a pleasure. Cleaning out the pantry is a great way to begin; put the clutter questions you learned in chapter three to the test. Discard expired and unused foods and vitamins, old pots and pans, broken appliances, and tarnished utensils. Definitely get rid of those warped, lidless plastic containers! By splurging for new ones, you can avoid a lot of frustration.

Proper shelving and containers should be set up to assist you in finding dry goods, canned foods, utensils, pots, pans, plastic containers, and more. Knowing where everything is will give you peace of mind and more quality time to do what you love. Add a light to the pantry and hang a wind chime from the ceiling to circulate the energy.

LEFT: A wooden butcher block and tall plants on a dining table disperse fast-moving energy in a long, narrow kitchen.

RIGHT: Pastel tiles and vibrant flowers embellish this cheerful kitchen. Hang pots and pans high over the center island and not directly overhead.

Do not place the garbage can in a prominent corner of the kitchen. Instead, hide it inside the pantry or under the sink. Make sure it has a lid to contain the dirty energy. Take the garbage out as often as possible. In addition, cleaning supplies, mops, brooms, and chemicals should be kept in a cabinet, not in view. Keep trash cans away from your side door; do not allow them share a wall with your stove.

lively kitchen décor

Here are some recommendations that will add cheerful colors and delightful smells to your kitchen:

- Paint the cabinets a vibrant color or stencil them with floral, nature, or food designs.
- Install tile with soothing colors depicting plants, flowers, and herbs above your sink and stove.
- Display colorful china, glassware, vases, pottery, and other cookware in open or glass cabinets.
- Arrange bowls and baskets of fruit symbolizing abundance and a cornucopia.
- Use spices, candles, and herbs to infuse wonderful aromas.

take action now

1. Place a convex mirror, plant, or barrier between your sink and stove if they are across from or next to one another to stabilize the fire/water energy.

2. Remove water and knives from the stove and hang a wind chime above your head.

3. Clear clutter off of and out of the refrigerator.

4. Clear off the countertops and pantry.

5. Place your garbage can out of view and buy a lid for it.

6. Add plants, flowers, light, and color to the space. Buy colorful dishtowels to get the process started.

7. Remember to energize the kitchen in terms of the bagua. If it is in your Wealth center, add a fountain, but do not place it near the stove.

8. Create a collage. The kitchen is a great place for a Health manifestation board. Use pictures of healthy fruits and vegetables, a favorite spa, an exercise activity, or physically and emotionally fit people who inspire you. Place it where you can see it everyday.

the dining room

What better place can you eat, drink, and be merry than in the dining room? It welcomes you whether you are sharing an intimate meal, enjoying a family dinner, eating solo, or entertaining a large party. Creating a multi-functional space will bring you, your family, and your guests much pleasure. Depending on the time of year and your mood or style, the room can exude a casual, fun, festive, elegant, or romantic flavor. The colors of the china, the shape and size of the table, the tablecloth and napkins, the stemware and flatware, the centerpiece, the lighting, and the greenery all affect the energy and decor. With a few quick variations, you can transform your surroundings into the dining experience you desire.

Regrettably, these days, the dining room is utilized only on special occasions. Most people are so hurried that a quick bite at the breakfast table is all the dining they allow themselves. Feng shui encourages you to use your dining room on a daily basis. You can create serenity and health by infusing it with positive energy. Pamper yourself physically and emotionally by sitting comfortably, nourishing your body, and connecting with your loved ones.

You'll discover that using your dining room every night offers many benefits. It affords you relaxation, connection, proper digestion, and positive family interaction. Gathering around the dinner table helps you to disconnect from a hectic day and to begin the inner process of slowing down before bed. To ease into a peaceful mood, turn on soft background music and create mood lighting with candles and colored lamps. Hopefully, the aroma of the food will whet your appetite.

The individual acts of setting the table, lighting candles, and serving the food contribute to a unified household. During meals, turn off the television and put down the newspaper. Tune out the world, if only for an hour or two, so you can listen genuinely and share openly. Giving thanks at dinner helps you to stay present and to cultivate an attitude of gratitude for all you have. For instance, each person can share three aspects of life for which they are grateful. Why not start with the delicious food you are about to eat, your family, and the shelter of your home?

RIGHT: The warm, rich color of red in the dining room stimulates engaging dinner talk and is superb for entertaining guests. The dimming effect of the chandelier and wall sconces creates an enchanting dinnertime mood.

dining room colors
The best colors for the dining room are beige, cream, green, blue, and soft pastels such as lavender, pink, peach, and apricot. Add bright yellows, oranges, and warm reds to stimulate the palate. Wallpaper, stencils, sponging, and faux finishes create additional texture.

the dining room table

The dining room table is the main piece of furniture in your dining room, the surface that holds your food, dinnerware, and decorations. The shapes, sizes, and materials you place on and around it create a specific energy. In general, a sturdy table with strong legs is best. If your table wobbles as you eat, you may be so annoyed that your digestion and conversation will suffer.

Place your dining room table in the middle of the room. This allows people to walk around the table and to get in and out of their chairs with ease. The shape and size of the dining room may dictate where you place it. If the size and shape of the table and room allow, try placing a rectangular table across the room rather than lengthwise, which is the natural inclination. Sometimes, a long table produces aggressive energy. If it is pointing towards you as you enter, you may feel uncomfortable and want to leave the room immediately. I have found that people sometimes avoid eating in the dining room simply because they are affected by this forceful energy.

designing your table and chairs

The shape and size of your dining room table creates different energy patterns in the room. Round or oval tables are optimal, encouraging energy to circle around the table, producing a sense of balance and harmony. Each seat receives equal prominence, which creates unity in the home. Rectangular and square tables work, provided that they have rounded corners and edges; the sharp, cutting energy from pointed edges encourages irritation and ill health while eating. You can soften the edges of all dining room furniture by using a silk tablecloth.

In addition, a rectangular table creates a spot for a person to sit at the "head" of the table. This shape gives power to the head of the household, especially if a larger chair symbolizing strength accompanies it. However, it can also

ABOVE: A tablecloth is a great solution for a rectangular dining table, softening its sharp edges. The light fixture and upward-facing palm break up oppressive energy created by the beams overhead.

holiday decorations

The dining table sets the tone for holidays throughout the year. Participate in the change of seasons by varying the colors of the tablecloth, the objects in the centerpiece, the flowers and plants, and the dinnerware. Pay homage to spiritual and cultural traditions by decorating your table with specific symbols and objects. Start a custom with your children by adorning the dining table with decorations for a particular holiday or season every few months.

cause inferiority in the other members sitting at the table. Consider your family unit when purchasing a new dining table to see which shape will promote the best connection.

Wooden tables are strong and stable. Wood brings in nature energy, grounds the food, and warms the space. If your old wooden table needs a fresh look, stain it with a new finish or paint it an antique white or a muted color such as green, blue, or light red. Tables with hard surfaces such as marble, granite, metal, wrought iron, and glass will accelerate energy. To soften sharp edges and slow the energy, cover it with a tablecloth, runner, or place mats.

BELOW: A round dining table promotes family harmony and allows energy to freely circulate around the diners.

A comfortable chair encourages leisurely dining. You want to lounge over a sumptuous meal enjoying food, drink, and stimulating conversation. Sturdy chairs with a solid back will support you; add seat cushions for additional comfort and color. Ensure that the view from each chair is a spectacular one, both inviting and pleasing to the eye. Another creative possibility is to let each family member place a beloved object or piece of art in the sight line from his or her favorite seat. However, don't create aesthetic disharmony.

dining room energy

As you know, plants and flowers add harmony, vitality, and color to any space. In your dining room, plants perched in corners and on top of china cabinets lift the energy. Placing trees such as a ficus or palm in corners creates a feeling of outdoor feasting. Fresh flowers or a plant worked into a centerpiece encourages harmony among diners. Silk flowers and plants also circulate energy and add beauty and color. Silk works especially well for lofty and hard-to-reach spaces.

Correct lighting boosts energy and establishes the mood of each meal. Traditionally, a lighting fixture such as a crystal, wooden, or wrought-iron chandelier hangs in the middle of the room. Do not hang it too low over the table or you may feel claustrophobic. Raise it up to make the room seem larger.

In general, feng shui recommends choosing a lighting fixture in which the bulbs and general shape point upward. You want the light to spread throughout the room and to bounce off the ceilings. Upward lighting lifts your spirits and says, "Chin up." It is not desirable to have strong beams of light pointing downward, exerting pressure on you as you eat. If you like, attach round, faceted crystals to the bottom of chandeliers to circulate energy in a balanced manner. Install a dimmer switch to the main lighting system and add small lamps with colored bulbs around the room to create a tranquil environment. Candles arranged on the table and sideboards will infuse additional warmth, romance, and ambiance.

serene artwork

Hang art depicting scenes and moods of ease and enjoyment that are gentle on your eyes. Landscapes, seascapes, and epicurean tableaux provide feast-enhancing images. If your dining room is small, try hanging art that has depth and creates a vista.

Large mirrors are very auspicious and considered good feng shui in the dining room. They add light, open up the space, and amplify food energy, multiplying your money. If you hang a mirror opposite a beautiful painting, it doubles the effect. Mirrors also encourage lively conversation and energize the room.

Murals can be another pleasing addition to the dining room, provided they depict a tranquil natural setting. If you have the money, hire a muralist to translate one of your favorite scenes onto your wall. Dedicate an entire wall to a French garden or a Tuscan countryside.

ABOVE: Fresh flowers and elegant candlesticks bring beauty into the dining room.

If you have always dreamed of a home overlooking an ocean or a mountain vista, a mural in the dining room is a great way to manifest it. When you are not eating in the dining room, use your inspiring space to accomplish work on creative projects.

dining room décor

The following feng shui recommendations will embellish the décor of your dining area:

- Make sure you love all the china, stemware, and crystal displayed in sideboards, buffets, and china cabinets.
- Add the fire energy of candles that illuminate your family and food. They come in many colors, shapes, and sizes providing a touch of elegance, radiance, and warmth.

BELOW: Colorful flowered rugs and artwork hearten this yellow dining area. Plush pillows soften sturdy chairs for hours of relaxed dining.

- Place an area rug underneath the dining table to add color, texture, and comfort.
- Accent your dining room with china in different colors to signify a change of season. For example, bring your pink china out in spring and your red, green and gold out in winter.
- Add happy photos of friends and family to a sideboard for connection.
- Use crystal candlesticks for fancy occasions and wooden or wrought-iron candlesticks for more casual dining.
- Use crystal stemware, bowls, vases, candelabras, and serving plates to add shimmer and iridescence to the dining room. In candlelight, crystal is especially magical. In addition, crystal spreads energy throughout the space.
- Add centerpieces incorporating fresh flowers or plants to energize the room and promote health. Candles, flowers, plants, bowls of fruit, and floating flowers create wonderful dining-table energy. You can mix and match unique pieces from different world cultures in styles ranging from pottery to delicate china to modern glass and silver pieces. Bowls of fruit represent opulence and fertility. Use real or attractive faux fruit to create a horn-of-plenty symbol.

the china cabinet

How many years has the same china sat in the same cabinet? Many times you don't even remember what you have because it only appears on special occasions. To begin the process, remove everything from your cabinet. Use the same questions you used in chapter three and store some of the china you remove to make room for new items. Clean the cabinet, the glass doors, and all of the china before putting it back. Make it sparkle. Then, arrange it in a completely new way. Bring fresh energy in by placing pieces in unique combinations. Changing the visual will stimulate your senses. The best advice I can give is to use your good china regularly. You deserve beauty at your fingertips all of the time.

ABOVE : Your favorite china and stemware add color and beauty to the dining table. Indulge yourself by using them regularly.

1. **Take a good look** at your dining table. Make sure it is sturdy and that there are no sharp corners pointing towards you as you eat. If necessary, soften the edges with tablecloth. Add colorful seat cushions to the chairs for extra comfort.

2. **Place something lovely** to look at in your line of vision as you sit in your regular chair.

3. **Allow natural sunlight** to shine into the room.

4. **Put your overhead light** fixture on a dimmer switch to enhance the ambiance.

5. **Add candles** for color, relaxation, fragrance, or romance.

6. **Hang a mirror** to expand a small, dark dining room.

7. **Place at least one large plant** in a corner and fresh flowers or a plant in the center of the table.

8. **Hang colorful artwork** that exhibits a feeling of abundance such as a bowl of fruit or a field of flowers. If your dining area feels claustrophobic, hang artwork with depth, creating the illusion of looking out a window. How about a mural?

the living room

Spending delightful moments with family and friends nurtures your soul. Whether you are enjoying a stimulating conversation, story telling, playing cards, listening to music, or dancing, the living room encourages leisure and festivity on many levels. After a satisfying meal, retiring to this cozy area is the natural choice. It is usually one of the largest rooms in the home, making it the perfect place to relax, socialize, and entertain.

Joyful experiences in the living room create the energy environment for many more in the future. Feng shui encourages you to dwell in every area of the home. A room that feels "lived in" is much more inviting than one rarely visited. Energy increases in an environment where people are present. The energies of activities and interactions that occur in a space are absorbed by that space's walls, furniture, carpet, and objects. To invite connection, introduce a piano for after-dinner song and dance or play games in which everyone can participate. Feel free to include quiet activities such as reading, writing, painting, and sewing to harmonize the energy.

Your guests can discover much about you, your spirit, and passions from the décor of your living room. It is an excellent area to show off unique items from a trip abroad or work by a local artist, as well as handcrafted

objects or family heirlooms. Exhibiting personal, cultural, and traditional art and mementos reveals your personality and interests. These objects spark interesting and lively conversations when entertaining. Displaying meaningful photographs of family events, vacations, and celebrations such as weddings, birthdays, anniversaries, and graduations fills the space with love and positive memories.

ABOVE: Energy easily flows around a circular ottoman while the fire, natural light, healthy trees, and mirrors enhance a comfortable seating area.

RIGHT: A L-shaped sofa of soft cotton provides a wonderful spot to relax and unwind. The sofa's position against the wall offers support and protection, providing those seated with a comfortable view of people entering the room.

an enticing sofa

The sofa is often the main feature of a living room, so it is important that you love the color, shape, size, and fabric of yours. Of course, comfort is essential to a fabulous sofa. An overstuffed, soft, cozy one will bring you, your family, and your guests endless pleasure. It provides the perfect spot for an intimate rendezvous or playtime with the kids. Shop wisely, testing different sofas before you purchase one.

Natural fibers are best. Soft cottons, linens, denims, velvet, damasks, and flannels work well. Unfortunately, a leather couch doesn't allow energy to circulate. Basically, the criterion is whether or not the fabric feels glorious to the touch. If you love your sofa but desire a new variation, purchase a slipcover. You will be amazed at the complete makeover in look, feel, and color. To create a new appearance for winter, choose a deeper color; select a brighter one for the summer. Simply adding new, colorful pillows can give your sofa the zest you desire.

seating arrangements for optimal flow

The proper position for your sofa will enhance power and harmony in the living room. When reclining on the main sofa, you should be able to see the door. In this way, the front of the sofa is "inviting" you and your guests to sit down when you enter. If you cannot see the door, hang a mirror across from it so that you can see when anyone comes in. Make sure the sofa isn't too close to the door so it doesn't block the flow of energy.

A sofa backed by a wall provides stability and protection for those seated on it. If your sofa is positioned in the middle of the room or backs up to a window, simulate a wall by placing a narrow table behind it with plants on top. Trees, either live or silk, will also do the job. You can achieve balance by arranging seating in round, semicircular, or square formations. As a result, everyone can easily see each other, enhancing conversation and a sense of community.

living room colors

Many different colors and textures work well in the living room. Neutrals such as beige, tan, and cream or calming colors such as green and blue provide a pleasing base. Yellow and orange stimulate the energy, while red, maroon, and purple warm the room. You can add accent colors in pillows, throws, rugs, drapes, artwork, lampshades, and candles. Be careful not to use too much black because it absorbs light instead of reflecting it.

ABOVE: A mirror placed over the mantel is beneficial, providing a gentle cooling effect for the fire energy.

LEFT: Vivid pastels on the walls, furniture, and rugs brighten the space. The artwork's rosy pink floral motif and the fresh bouquets on mantle and coffee table create loving energy.

To complement the sofa, add a side table, coffee table, small bookcase, or ottoman. A loveseat or chaise lounge is also a good addition. For the best feng shui, select rounded furniture with rounded cushions. Add a plant to the coffee table and intriguing books for your guests to flip through.

The following seating arrangements can be utilized for the living room, den, or study:

- Create a square shape with two sofas directly across from each other and chairs on either side with a coffee table in the middle (see page 226).
- Create a semicircle around a fireplace or entertainment center with a sofa and a few chairs. Place a table in the middle (see page 222).
- Create a semicircle with an L-shaped sectional by adding a chair to balance the shorter side and a table for the center (see page 223).

the fireplace

Fire generates warmth, love, and kinship for everyone in the home. Whether you enjoy reading, writing, needlepoint, or puzzles, the fireplace provides a focal point for family to gather around. It sparks conversation and connection. Why not schedule a few evenings per month where everyone congregates around the fireplace to interact with one another in a creative way? An "open mike" night where everyone takes a turn can be lots of fun, filling the house with laughter and joy.

The following are a few tips for the fireplace:

- Sprinkle a few drops of essential oil on a log before burning it. This adds a wonderful fragrance. Oils such as sandalwood, rosemary, cinnamon, rosewood, orange, rose, and lemon add a delicious fragrance to the living room.
- Place plants inside the fireplace when it is not in use to harmonize the fire energy.
- Add a water element, such as a water fountain or vase full of fresh flowers, to subdue the fire energy if your fireplace

is in the center of the home. This water helps to ease tension between family members and stabilize your finances.

- Hang a colorful piece of art or a decorative mirror over the mantel. Anything that you place in front of the mirror will be multiplied. Try a plant in a gold pot.
- Remove photos of loved ones from the mantel. Fire energy is too hot for friends and family.
- Add candles, fresh flowers, plants, colorful objects, and mementos to the mantelpiece.

the entertainment center

Years ago, people used to gather around the fire; today, the entertainment center is the main attraction. With VCRs and DVDs for movie rentals and cable supplying hundreds of channels, the television has all but replaced family communication. At night, the remote is clicking away while everyone attempts to agree on a program. To maximize interaction, place the television inside a cabinet or drape a piece of fabric on top to discourage excessive use. If you see the television the moment you walk into the room, the odds are that you will turn it on automatically. In this case, the concept of "out of sight, out of mind" works well with feng shui. Use wooden cabinets to bring in nature energy.

Stereos, CD players, DVDs, and all electronics should also be placed inside a cabinet to contain the electromagnetic energy. You can add plants to the top of the entertainment center to soften the energy of such a large piece of furniture. If you have additional space for personal items, display photos and mementos on the shelves. You can install lighting inside the cabinets to illuminate beautiful artifacts.

sunken living rooms

You must pay special attention to sunken living rooms because positive energy from the main level travels downward to the sunken area and accumulates on the floor. To elevate the energy, hang pictures up high so your gaze stays at the same height as the art on the main level. Add tall plants in colorful pots and create lighting that points towards the ceiling. Tall furniture and standing lamps provide height as well. Hang round, faceted

LEFT: This square seating arrangement encourages interaction. Simply opening doors and adding plants invites nature's healing energy into the room.

crystals in each corner a few inches from the ceiling to keep the energy rotating up high. In addition, you can hang a round, faceted crystal to the bottom of any chandelier for a similar effect.

As you know, clearing clutter is a surefire method to raise energy. Peruse your book collection and discard books that no longer represent you and your life's direction. Pick up odds and ends from the floor to avoid pulling the energy downward. Sort through your CDs, videos, software, and video games to see which ones you want to give away. You can clear space for new ones and generate good karma simultaneously.

high ceilings

High ceilings offer a light, airy, and spacious feeling to the living room. However, you may also feel slightly lost and unprotected. The energy tends to scatter up high, causing a sense of instability. Bringing the energy down to a normal height will restore a safe and grounded feeling.

Solutions

- Lay a rug or carpet on the floor to ground the energy.
- Create a false ceiling by hanging large artwork around the room at the same height. Use the top of a door frame or window to establish an appropriate height.
- Use stenciling or molding to "lower" the ceiling.
- Use large armoires and bookcases to create a focal line of normal height.
- Hang a chandelier eleven to thirteen feet above the floor.
- Stabilize the space by placing large pieces of furniture against the walls.

low ceilings

Although low ceilings offer security, intimacy, and warmth, they can also make you feel constricted, oppressed, and claustrophobic. Low ceilings tend to propel energy towards the floor.

Solutions

- Paint the room and the ceiling a light color.
- Use lamps that send light up towards the ceiling.

the bagua and the living room

The living room is usually one of the largest rooms in the home, and this makes it an excellent place to overlay the bagua. If you have a missing energy center in your home or if one of your bathrooms is located in an important energy center, strengthen those centers of your living room with plants and light. You can use the layering technique to achieve your goals. In addition to energizing the corner of the house that correlates to the center you want to stimulate, you should also energize the corresponding corner of the living room. For example, if you are concentrating on changing your career, energize the front middle of the living room with a water fountain. Remember that when applying the bagua to an individual room, you want to overlay it from the point of view of the door to that room (see chapters five and six for further enhancements).

- Paint clouds on the ceiling to give the illusion of being outdoors.
- Avoid dark colors on both walls and ceilings because they will make the room feel even smaller and the ceiling even lower.
- Place smaller pieces of furniture in the room to make the space seem larger.

windows

Windows can usher in sunlight, fresh air, and positive energy. However, if you have too many, you may find it difficult to relax; energy may fly in and out of the windows without circulating through the room and home. Large windows and sliding glass doors cause the same problem. They do not allow the room to retain the energy essential for healthy living.

Solutions
- Hang a round, faceted crystal in each large window to slow down energy.
- Place or hang plants in the window or between two windows to disperse the energy.
- Hang drapes. Open them during the day to allow sunlight to bathe the room.
- Notice if your front door is opposite a large living room window. As discussed in the foyer section, hang a crystal between the door and the window to stop the energy from the front door energy going straight out the window.
- Open east-facing windows to bring in fortunate energy.

exposed beams and protruding corners

As discussed in the bedroom section, overhead beams exert pressure downward. Be aware of them in your living area and do not place your sofa or chairs beneath them. If your ceilings are higher than fifteen feet, the pressure exerted by the beams will be less potent. Obviously, the lower the beam, the more it can affect your health and relationships (refer to pages 189-190 for complete solutions for exposed beams.)

Sharp edges on all furniture including side tables, coffee tables, desks, armoires, and bookshelves should be moderated with silk tablecloths or live or silk plants. Likewise, corners of protruding walls require softening to disperse their sharp energy. Do not place the sofa or chairs in the direct line of a protruding corner.

Solutions

- Place a large bushy plant at the corner to disperse sharp energy.
- Hang a crystal so that it is positioned one-third of the way down the sharp edge or corner.

living room furnishings

Traditional furniture such as an armoire, bookcase, or entertainment center accents your living room seating arrangements. To introduce different shapes and sizes, add a sculpture, a piano, large globe, standing lamp, or mirror. Mix and match different-sized artwork as well. Fringe, tassels, and crystals can be sewn on lampshades, tablecloths, and drapes for texture. Of course, you can elevate the positive energy by placing plants and lights in the corners. Incense or fragrant room spray will add a pleasant aroma.

Bookcases keep reading material handy, and this can inspire storytelling. For stability, place book-shelves on large walls. The spines of the books should be flush with the edge of the shelf to elim-inate cutting and protruding energy produced by each shelf. Another solution is to add glass doors to the bookcases. Keep inspirational literature, poetry, and biographies of successful people in view; cultural and travel books will summon the energy of the world. As a rule, avoid lining up too many large pieces of furniture against the same wall. This leads to stagnant energy.

Remember that antiques carry the energy of the people who owned them into your space. You can clean your antiques by waving a stick of sandal-wood incense around and inside of them. If the antique is from a relative who was successful, happy, and full of love, then it is good feng shui

stimulating decor

How long have your furniture, books, art and mementos sat in the same place? People who have lived in the same home for many years tend to be crea-tures of habit, becoming complacent with surround-ings that were decorated and furnished years ago. Unfortunately, after a certain period of time, your environment ceases to inspire or stimulate you. You pass by the same picture day after day and no longer take notice. To promote change, create new stimuli by moving at least twenty objects to new locations. Experiment by moving vases, pottery, picture frames, lamps, furniture, and plants.

and can deliver good fortune. If not, it may be emanating negativity and should be cleaned, donated, refinished, or repainted to uplift the energy.

Rugs help define a space and establish color, comfort, and warmth in the environment. If you have an open space meant for both your living and dining room, you can create a room within a room by placing a rug in one area with seating around it. If your living room has hardwood floors, a rug will give you the opportunity to sit or lie on the ground, especially if you add large pillows for extra padding.

During this process, notice if there are items in your home that you adored five, ten, or twenty years ago that no longer fit your style and taste. Would you buy these items in these colors with these patterns today? Ideally, you want to surround yourself with the things you love. However, you need not purchase all new items. Get creative by changing fabrics, painting furniture, and adding new colors to freshen up the look. Your goal is to be able to sit anywhere in your home and love what you see.

ABOVE LEFT: Display treasured photos, books, and unique collectibles in a bookcase to ignite engaging conversations about your passions and interests.

ABOVE: Brightly hued pottery, rugs, pillows, and blankets add culture, texture, and color to the living room.

a place to replenish your spirit

Create a room or nook where you can reflect, be quiet, go inside, and get centered. In your daily life, you have so much to think about and to do. Between work, children, errands, and meals, you hardly have a moment for yourself. This is why you must have a special place to renew your connection with your inner self and spirit. You might convert an attic or guest room or simply create a corner or window seat in your living area that is dedicated to self-nourishment. Hanging a screen, beads, or billowy curtain will help emphasize the importance of the environment as a place of solitude.

take action now

1. **Position your sofa** to invite guests to sit down. If your sofa is in the middle of the room, add a table behind it. Put a plant on the table for protection.

2. **Look for sharp edges and exposed beams.** Move your sofa to a different location or use the proper solutions to disperse negative energy.

3. **Energize** the most important centers in the room with a plant.

4. **Add a small water fountain** to the back left corner to boost your wealth.

5. **Place a mirror** behind a plant and fountain to double the positive energy.

6. **Make sure all photos represent positive memories** and self-esteem.

7. **Enclose or cover** your television and electronic equipment.

8. **Clear clutter** from bookshelves, cabinets, and closets.

9. **Remove pictures** of friends and family from the mantle.

10. **Add** a mirror, inspirational artwork, pillows, or candles for colorful décor.

This sacred space can be used to receive inner guidance and knowledge as well as to write, draw, paint, chant, play an instrument, or simply listen to birds sing outside. To set the mood for contemplation, meditation, or prayer, place pillows on the floor and set up an altar with spiritual objects. Creating an altar can be as simple as draping a small table with a special fabric. On top of the table, place items such as a scented candle, incense burner, essential oil diffuser, or natural objects like rocks and seashells that bring in the earth element. You can add plants and flowers for energy. Pictures of gardens, mountains, spiritual teachers, angels, or mentors impart a feeling of peace and harmony. Soft music and an insightful book will offer you inspiration.

LEFT: A quiet spot to sit surrounded by inspiring books, flourishing plants, and a spiritual anchor such as a golden Buddha make a delightful nook for peaceful contemplation and meditation.

RIGHT: This wooden water tank is converted into a soothing outdoor environment with plants, colorful pillows, and natural stones from the earth.

ten:

workplace and home office

a thriving career requires a harmonious, efficient, and well-organized work space. As you create an office with proper feng shui, professional opportunities and financial gain become more accessible. Creating momentum and motivation is the key to your success—and an inspiring workplace.

The office is the place to express your creativity and talent and, hopefully, to earn a fabulous living. "Visioneering" is a word I use to describe the idea of creating a vision for your entire life and putting a plan into motion to achieve it. Visioneering encompasses much more than working in a job to make ends meet. It unites intention, determination, action, and energy to convert your dreams and goals into reality. Feng shui is a natural complement to the visioneering process.

Decorating and energizing your office properly are important. Think of the hours that you spend at work; in some cases, people spend more than twelve a day in their office. You must create an environment that supports, empowers, and motivates you continually. Clarify your specific goals as you apply the principles of feng shui to your work space. What are your intentions for your present and future career? Does your office express your personality, professionalism, confidence, and work objectives? Keep in mind that the way you "show up" today determines your future achievements.

Whether you work from home or at an office, many of the enhancements will be the same. I recommend that you read the entire chapter to effectively apply the principles of feng shui to your particular environment. Now is the time to create an office that drives you towards the most satisfying career for you.

office colors

Bright, multicolored offices will enliven you and your projects. Begin with neutrals and add other colors to enhance your work environment. Add red and maroon to strengthen, motivate, and increase action. Yellow and orange create liveliness and cheerfulness. Blue and lavender soothe a stressful, hectic environment. Green is for balance, harmony, and new opportunities. Use accents of black and brown for stability. The powerful combination of red and gold promotes prosperity.

PREVIOUS PAGE: In the office, first impressions set the tone for extraordinary business. To encourage efficiency and success, keep your desk clutter-free, organized, and energized with plants and flowers.

efficiency, confidence, and organization

Organization tops the list for achieving productivity, and a clutter-free environment is key if you desire a clear vision for your career. When files, papers, and projects are scattered on the desk or floor, they send a message to your conscious and subconscious that you feel inundated. Stagnant energy sets in and projects come to a standstill. Remember, clutter creates undue stress and impedes your success, sending out a negative message to your potential clients and colleagues. Having a reputation for being disorganized is not helpful to your career, especially if you are in a leadership position. Instead, design the reputation you desire.

mobile clutter

As you know, people tend to accumulate clutter in their wallets, purses, and briefcases, which hinders personal feng shui. Throw out unnecessary receipts, trash, stale gum, hardened hand lotion, dried up pens, etc. Do not carry your money in dilapidated or dirty money holders. Your wallet should exude elegance and prosperity. In addition, organize papers, notepads, supplies, and your laptop computer in an orderly fashion in your briefcase. Write your career goals in red ink and place a copy inside your case to anchor them. To energize and multiply your riches, slip your paychecks into red envelopes for at least twenty-four hours before depositing them into your bank account. Always try to carry enough money in your wallet to promote a feeling of safety and abundance. I keep an imitation million dollar bill in my organizer and on my Wealth manifestation board at all times.

The entrance to your workspace should be free of obstructions. The door must open wide for all of your opportunities to fly in easily and speedily. Your coworkers and clients will be thankful, too. What is your office communicating about you? Is it the image you want to convey? The first impression of your office can affect your daily performance as well as the way others view you.

Perhaps you are one of those people who have "organized clutter." You may try to fool yourself by arranging it neatly in notebooks, files, and bookshelves, but it still weighs you down. You must remove or store old or unsuccessful work projects. Create forward momentum and lure new creativity by removing anything in your office that had a negative outcome. Keep current projects in red folders and notebooks to promote rapid manifestation.

If the boss calls you in need of a quick answer, are you able to find important materials in a matter of seconds, or are you frantically searching for the one indispensable report? This type of incident, occurring again and again, could negatively influence a promotion. Are you committed to organizing your office yet?

removing clutter and confusion

- Clear clutter from the top of your desk. Remove everything from the surface of your desk, dust it, and start from scratch, placing items purposefully.
- Empty your drawers. Arrange pens, pencils, rubber bands, scissors, and paper clips in an organizing tray in the drawer.
- Fix broken items.
- Throw out dead flowers and plants.
- Clean out filing cabinets, bookshelves, and credenzas. Keep only active files and projects at hand. Store the infrequently referenced ones outside of your office.
- Remove items that you do not use.
- Remove everything from the floor. Set up storage bins, containers, filing cabinets, and shelving so that everything has a proper place.

optimal desk position

Your desk is the key to your productivity and success. A sizable, neatly arranged desk represents power and confidence; a tiny, disorderly one reflects feelings of anxiety and low self-esteem. What is your desk saying about you?

Oval or kidney-shaped desks are preferable since they are rounded. Avoid rectangular desks with sharp corners because you do not want sharp energy cutting into you for eight to twelve hours a day as you work. Your desk should have adequate surface space to comfortably accommodate your computer, phone, and paperwork, as well as a few personal items. A U-shaped desk keeps everything within arms' reach, contributing to your efficiency.

The power position for the desk is diagonally opposite from the door with your back to the wall or catty-corner to the wall. In this position, you have a large view of the room and the door. This gives you the security of knowing who is entering your office. It also affords you the opportunity to view an inspiring piece of artwork on the opposite wall. The desk should be placed far enough away from the wall that you can get in and out of your chair with ease. Also, make sure you have ample legroom. Bumping into a wastebasket or other office equipment everyday is bad feng shui (see above, A).

Computer, printer, phone, and fax cables are unattractive. Enclose them in a plastic tube purchased at an office supply store. You may want to wrap fabric around the tube to conceal it. You can place plants in front of the desk to further camouflage the cables.

RIGHT: Illustration A shows the best position for your desk; positions indicated in B and C should be avoided if possible.

FAR RIGHT: A pleasing view enhances creative vision as you work. Positive energy from bright colors and natural light stimulates your mind and emotional well being.

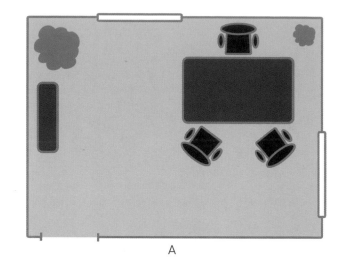

A

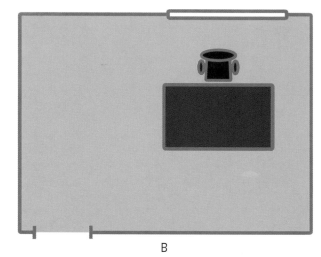

B

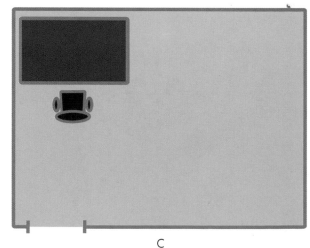

C

poor desk positions

Try to avoid these desk positions:

Back to a Large Window

When your back faces a large window, your strength, creativity, and moneymaking energy will flow outside. Your energy must be protected and contained by a solid wall to support your endeavors. If there is no alternative position available for your desk, create a barrier behind you with a filing cabinet, credenza, small table, or bookcase. Put a plant on top of the item you choose (see B, page 238).

Direct Line with the Door

With your desk in this position, the energy coming from another office or hallway can cause agitation and discomfort. You may find yourself unable to concentrate and yearn to leave your desk. To correct and slow down the energy, create a barrier between your desk and the door. Use a credenza, small bookcase, filing cabinet or small table for this purpose. Place a plant on top of the desk to disperse incoming energy. Hang a round, faceted crystal halfway between the door and the desk, two inches below the top of the door frame (see C, page 238).

Desk against the Wall

In this position, your back faces the majority of the room and the door. This causes two problems. First, when facing a wall, you encounter a literal "wall" or obstacle each time you lift your head from the computer; this can block your inspiration. Second, you may feel uneasy at your desk if people can sneak up and peer over your shoulder. This lack of privacy and concentration eventually affects your productivity. Being aware of what is happening behind you is necessary for a feeling of confidence, efficiency, and power. Also, when your back is to the door, you may be subliminally sending the wrong message to your coworkers. They may feel you are unavailable and uninterested in being part of a team. Unfortunately, many offices have built-in desk units facing a wall. To correct this, place a small mirror above the desk so that you can see who or what is behind you. You can also hang art, such as a seascape or landscape, at eye level to encourage creative vision. Do not place a mirror reflecting you at your desk because it will multiply your workload. Less work with more money is the objective (see C, page 238).

RIGHT: Give your desk a commanding position by securing a wide view of the room and door. Trees and plants work wonderfully to diffuse excessive energy rushing in through large windows, which may be unsettling.

complementary office furniture

If you have ample room, set up an area in your office for clients and coworkers to meet with you. Adding a couch, chairs, and a coffee table creates the opportunity for relaxed discussions and brainstorming sessions in a comfortable setting. Plants and colorful books related to your specific industry can go on the coffee table (see page 225 for proper seating arrangements). Do not allow filing cabinets and bookshelves to overpower the room. When you clear your clutter, decide what is absolutely necessary for you to have inside the office on a daily basis. Excessive furniture creates stagnant energy. Old files can be stored in boxes, in a filing cabinet outside the door, or in another location.

the right chair

Your chair should provide comfort and support; you will be sitting in it for many hours a day. A well-designed, ergonomically correct chair is best for proper posture and back support. This type of chair will reduce work injuries and increase productivity. For maximum comfort, your chair should be adjustable. Find one that can be raised, lowered, and tilted to fit your needs. A soft seat cushion is a lifesaver; head and armrests allow you to take a break. For easy movement, try a chair on wheels.

office décor

Invest time, energy, and love in your office and you will be generously rewarded. Often you are presented with a sterile space, and you simply move in without a second thought. By adding vibrant colors, personal items, and living energy to the environment, you allow your personality to shine through. It is important to create the energy of success and excitement by placing objects that uplift you and that stir your creative juices. Your office is your home away from home.

Hang an inspirational, colorful picture across from your desk. It should evoke images of achievement and endless possibilities for you. In addition, photos of loved ones, friends, or a favorite vacation spot bring connection into the workplace. Plants in the corners instill harmony. Fresh flowers on your desk add color, beauty, and fragrance.

If possible, avoid sitting under fluorescent lights. Halogen and incandescent bulbs are easier on the eyes; full-spectrum bulbs are your best choice. Of course, natural sunlight will uplift your energy and spirit. Why not take a walk during lunch to absorb a little more? You should also check your clocks. Be certain they work properly and are set to the correct time. Set them slightly ahead to improve your punctuality. If your clocks have stopped, your momentum at work may follow.

LEFT: Make colleagues feel at home: create a comfortable seating area for meetings and brainstorming sessions. Display unique artwork, attractive souvenirs, and collector's items to personalize your office and spark interesting conversation.

your achievements

Displaying indicators of your personal and professional accomplishments and successful projects such as certificates of excellence and college diplomas in your office surrounds you with an aura of confidence and self-worth. Articles written about you and your business should be visible and framed, preferably in red! These achievements are continually sending you and your visitors messages of credibility and merit. If you feel good about what you do, others will respect you. Update your walls with new accolades as you obtain them.

Remove items that remind you of unsuccessful businesses or projects. These objects subconsciously deplete you and create a feeling of inadequacy. Pending projects you expect to secure as well as future goals should be in full view or, if you need privacy, in a drawer. Focus on them for continued motivation; "breathe" them into your psyche every day. They serve as reminders of the career and life you are visioneering.

ABOVE: Experience the harmonious effect of nature's energy by incorporating plants in office décor, and opening windows in temperate weather.

OPPOSITE: Overlay the bagua on your desk to motivate you and energize your career.

In addition, remember to cut the cord from negative people who upset you. Feel free to do this as many times a day as necessary. Do not allow a boss, colleague, or even a client to get the best of you. For maximum energy, disconnect from depleting situations and infuse yourself with healthy, supportive ones. Refer to chapter two whenever you need to summon more positive energy into your daily schedule.

your computer and your health

Many people sit in front of a computer screen word processing, researching the Internet, creating graphs and charts, or entering numbers

 wealth and prosperity

fame and reputation

love and relationships

family

health

creativity and children

knowledge and wisdom

career

helpful people

the bagua at work

Apply the bagua in your office to create forward momentum for all of your projects. Start by placing a water fountain in the Wealth or Career center and plants in Relationships, Knowledge, and Helpful People centers. In addition, you can overlay the bagua on the surface of your desk. Orient it from where you sit, as if that were the front door. In this way, the Career center is located in the front middle of the desk. The following are suggestions for implementing the bagua on your desk. Use your imagination to create a few that suit you and your office specifically:

- **Back left corner (Wealth)**—Place an expensive item, such as a crystal vase, antique clock, or valuable pen to represent your fortune. Something gold is very fortuitous. A small water fountain works on a larger desk.

- **Back right (Relationships)**—Place flowers, a picture of you and a loved one, or an uplifting quote.
- **Back middle (Fame)**—Place a lamp or red candle. Your business cards or name and title plate will promote your position.
- **Middle left (Family)**—Place a picture of your family or a gift from a family member.
- **Middle right (Creativity)**—Place a colorful mug or bright notes with inspirational sayings or affirmations.
- **Front left (Knowledge)**—Place books and reference materials.
- **Front right (Helpful People)**—Place the telephone, projects, or clients files.
- **Front center (Career)**—Place the computer with a decorative mouse pad or notebook.

for countless hours each day. Electromagnetic fields emitted by computers can cause headaches and reduce your ability to concentrate. A radiation screen and a plant placed next to the computer will help counteract harmful effects. Sit as far away from the screen as possible and shut it off when you're not using it. To minimize glare, tilt the monitor back and slightly below eye level. Make it a priority to get up from your desk every so often to give your eyes a rest. On an organizational level, clear clutter from your hard drive and downloaded documents. Delete old files to open up more space in your computer for new projects. Archive important documents on a floppy disk to ensure their survival.

 # the office at large

If you are the office manager at your company or you own your own business, you have the opportunity to apply the principles of feng shui to the entire space. Even if you only have control over your own desk or cubicle, you have a choice of many enhancements to create a lively and comfortable work area. Feel free to modify the information from the previous chapters to fit your office space.

Just as you did at home, you should give special attention to energizing the front entrance. Make it as welcoming as possible outside and inside; colorful visuals and pleasing aromas support employee satisfaction and cheerful clients. Even a few treats such as mints, candy, fresh fruit, and drinks can boost business meetings. Energize the bathrooms, too. In general, add lots of plants to produce harmony amongst the staff. The following are recommendations for an open office, conference room, and individual cubicle:

open office arrangements

An office in which everyone works in the same area leaves little room for privacy and individuality. In some companies, only the higher-ups have private offices. In some instances, you have no control over the direction your desk faces since many open-office configurations contain built-in desks. In general, desks that face each other invite collaboration. However, having your own personal space is important.

ABOVE: An inspiring collage prompts innovative ideas for current projects; the oval conference table encourages successful teamwork.

Using a little ingenuity, you can create a protective wall on your desk with the computer, lamp, plant, and photos. You need to express your individuality even though you are part of a team. If the office is cold and void of spirit, do your best to bring in color, plants, and lovely images. Place them in your sight line to stimulate and motivate you. If feasible, avoid sitting near the restroom because you want to avoid toilet energy traveling towards you.

conference rooms

Decorate your conference room to encourage successful meetings. A round or oval table promotes unity, creativity, and a sense of teamwork. As with a round dining table, energy can circulate around the room and the table easily. A rectangular or square table promotes efficiency as long as the corners are softened. U-shaped conference tables allow people to see one another easily and, at the same time, provide a focal point at the top of the U

247

for presentations. Place plants and trees in the corners to sustain harmony among employees and potential clients. Open the windows to let in fresh air and sunlight. Hang inspiring and colorful artwork and indicators of your company's accomplishments and goals on the walls.

the cubicle

Every space deserves attention and love, especially a cubicle. When you give it a helping hand by introducing positive elements, you will find that you take more pride in your work and feel happier, too. Apply the principles of feng shui to your cubicle to create a pleasing environment and personalize it to make it feel more like home. Here are a few suggestions:

- Construct a protective "wall" behind you with a small filing cabinet, bookcase, or table if your desk faces a partition. This barrier helps to create more privacy because people will stop before entering your personal space. Place a small mirror above your desk so that you can see who is coming.
- Use a comfortable chair with proper support even if your space is limited.
- Add an inspiring picture that has depth in front of you to open up the space. If a corkboard hangs above the desk, decorate it with pictures of friends and family, colorful photos of scenic vistas, and inspiring quotes in addition to your "to do" lists.
- Add silk or fresh flowers or a plant.
- Bring a few mementos from home for your desk.
- Place a foot massager under your desk for relaxing sensations in the midst of your workday.
- Play soft music for privacy and pleasure.

ABOVE: Perk up a cubicle with a collage filled with photos of friends and family, and creative representations of wishes for the present and future. Hang pictures of nature scenes at eye level to give yourself a "view" and open the way for creative vision. Add a healthy plant to diffuse harmful electromagnetic rays emitted by the computer screen.

the home office

Whether you work part-time for additional income, full-time as an entrepreneur, or just desire an inviting setting to pay bills

BELOW: Backed by a solid wall, a sturdy wooden desk provides strength and support to accomplish your goals. Red and gold attract prosperity and create forward momentum.

and write emails, you can dedicate a special area in your home to accomplish these goals. Many of you are in professions, such as teaching or accounting, where you inevitably bring projects home to complete at night or on weekends. By creating a workspace that unites the efficiency of an office with the personal comforts of home, you can fulfill all of your needs.

One of the wonderful aspects about a home office is that you have total control over style, décor, and placement. Instead of streamlined, factory-style furniture, you have the opportunity to choose warm, inviting pieces that match or complement the rest of your home. You can also conduct your business in a more personalized way, surrounded by family photos and cherished belongings that inspire you. Of course, to function properly, you will also need to incorporate organizational elements and electronic equipment into the space.

Many of the enhancements for the home office are similar to those for the workplace. For example, the placement of your desk is the same. Ideally, you want your desk to be facing into the rest of your home. This position allows you to observe the varied activities taking place in your home and helps your family to feel included in your work. Remember not to place your desk underneath an exposed beam or to allow it to share a wall with a toilet.

Open the windows and drapes to allow fresh air and natural daylight to stream in. General lighting should be soft and should come from different sources. Install a dimmer to an overhead light fixture to soften the beam coming down on your head. Supplemental lighting such as wall sconces or standing lamps will bounce light off the ceiling, uplifting the energy. You can adjust a desk lamp to aid in reading and writing. When possible, use full-spectrum bulbs and, of course, add plants to the corners.

location within the home

When integrating an office into your home environment, consider what you need to be happy, motivated, and productive. The room you dedicate to your office depends on the type of work you do and your personality. If you are an artist, composer, writer, or someone who can only concentrate when it is quiet, your office should be located towards the back of the home and away from street noise. For extra tranquility, open a window or

ABOVE: Decorate your home office with less "office like" furnishings, such as an appealing lamp, organizational baskets, and attractive, movable filing cabinets.

LEFT: An office located at the front of the home is perfect for receiving clients. It is best to move your desk if your back is to a window. However, when there is no alternative, a plant-topped credenza placed behind you will stop your prosperity energy from escaping out the window.

door to look out upon your garden. Let nature inspire you. An outside waterfall can provide hours of peace.

On the other hand, if your business requires clients to visit your work space, you want your office near the front of your home. A window looking out on the front yard allows you to see clients approaching and to greet them immediately. Be sure your address is clearly marked and the entrance is uncluttered and attractive. Remember, you are making a first impression. A separate entrance to your work space is ideal to avoid client traffic through your main living area. Arrange proper seating inside your office so people feel comfortable and at ease while meeting with you.

the personal touch

One of your objectives may be to design the room to look less like an office. In doing so, feel free to cover or hide your computer, fax machine, printer, scanner, or other electronic equipment in a handsome cupboard or to drape them with fabric when not in use. Shelving and storage is essential in facilitating a clutter-free room and desk. Rather than using more traditional organizers, purchase colored containers, bowls, baskets, and boxes for papers and supplies. To maintain an organized and clean environment, you may want to invest in cabinets with doors. Closing the cabinet doors helps to keep office chaos to a minimum. It looks better, too.

You may also want to conceal those unattractive metal filing cabinets. One option is to purchase a filing cabinet on wheels that can be tucked away in a closet when not in use. Another alternative is to place a round piece of wood on top of a low filing cabinet to create a table. First, measure the top of the cabinet. Purchase a piece of round wood large enough to cover it. Place a tablecloth over the entire cabinet, adding a lamp and a plant. You will have a perfect side table to complement a sofa or chair. You can also find filing cabinets made of wicker, wood, or decorative metal design.

be ready for the opportunity of a lifetime

Imagine that an influential person in your industry is coming to give you an amazing opportunity or job. With this fortunate break, you will be incredibly successful in your career. Are you comfortable inviting this person into your office? This is the first impression he or she will have of you. Your office must project your capability, organization, efficiency, power, and creativity. Give this person every reason to give you the opportunity of a lifetime. For example, suppose your goal is to write a film that Steven Spielberg would direct, and he has agreed to meet with you. Would you and your office give the impression that you have perfected your craft? Does it show that you are focused, impassioned, and able to communicate your vision? Create an office that emanates success and confidence. As you work and marinate in this positive environment, you never know who might walk through the door.

Spread items that make you feel rich and successful throughout your office. An elegant statue, expensive pen, antique lamp, or notable book collection creates a feeling of abundance. Place one in your Wealth center along with a water fountain for increased prosperity.

creating healthy boundaries

Being close to family is a wonderful asset in having a home office. You have no commute, and you have the pleasure of home-cooked meals. However, sometimes personal interruptions make it difficult to accomplish any serious work. If possible, install a dedicated phone line for business calls. Ask your family to respect your work hours as if you were at an outside office.

On the other end of the spectrum, you cannot allow work to take over your entire life or home. Being self-employed gives you the opportunity to work at all hours of the night and weekend, which is unhealthy. Give yourself a break in order to start fresh on Monday morning. A good way to wind down from a workday is to cover your computer with fabric, indicating it's time to go "home."

take action now

1. **Place your desk** in the power position, soften sharp corners, and hang inspirational art across from your desk.

2. **Hang a small mirror** above your desk to see who is behind you if your back is to the door.

3. **Hang a picture at eye level** if your desk faces a wall. The picture should have depth to expand your creative vision. A scenic calendar or framed magazine clipping is an inexpensive option.

4. **Add plants** to the corners.

5. **Place a water fountain** in the Wealth or Career center of the office.

6. **Display your accomplishments** and goals in red frames.

7. **Assemble a manifestation board or notebook.** Place it where you can see it everyday.

feng shui tips

creating environments that empower is becoming second nature to you. The following pages are filled with important and playful methods to further integrate feng shui into your life and surroundings. These tips and shortcuts will accelerate your good fortune in wonderful ways.

tip one—feng shui and your life

Feng shui is an ever-evolving journey. During the transformation process, your desires, goals, and values may shift direction. As your dreams and goals manifest in one area of your life, you may feel compelled to switch focus. For instance, after creating a stable and loving relationship with your companion, you may want to concentrate on a career change or another area of your life.

Use your intuition to determine if the feng shui enhancements are working for you. If your life is not progressing as fast as you would like, be patient. Energy moves in mysterious ways. Some people get substantial results immediately; others notice subtle shifts over a few months. Everyone's life path is different, and energy responds to each person in a unique way. As you know, your personal karma plays a role.

Feng shui is one of many tools to use throughout your life. However, you must still do the work necessary to facilitate change. Pursuing job opportunities, communicating honestly with your partner, spending quality time parenting your children, and staying healthy are your responsibilities. A crystal, plant, or water fountain will support you and create momentum. These enhancements may start the ball rolling, but you must follow through.

The great news is that feng shui rotates the negative aspects out of your life so that the positive ones can come shining through. At times, implementing feng shui in a certain area may seem to manifest as a loss before you experience the opportunity. For example, you decide to energize your relationship center. Your desire is to get married, but your companion is lukewarm to the idea. In essence, you want a commitment sooner rather than later. However, sometimes the universe has different plans for you. By energizing the Love center, your relationship might dissolve in order for you to find and marry a more suitable person. Be open for the most fitting opportunity to come your way. You never know how or when it will show up.

PREVIOUS PAGE: A courtyard is a perfect place to sit and write down your goals and visualize fortuitous outcomes; this one, with its exquisite fountain surrounded by lush flowers and plants, overflows with abundant, prosperous energy.

tip two—your instincts

You must feel comfortable and content in your surroundings. By introducing feng shui solutions and enhancements at an even pace, you can determine how they are affecting your life. You may want to start off with one or two enhancements in each room or center before diving into five or six.

My suggestion is to try applying feng shui principles to your home and see what happens. Keep in mind that energy takes time to shift, so stick with the adjustments for at least three or four months to get the results you're looking for. You must balance the idea of creating good energy in your space with your personal taste and comfort. For instance, if you move your bed to a position that should produce good feng shui but you are sleeping poorly, change it back to the original position. Ultimately, it should feel good to you. You know yourself better than anyone.

Similarly, if you are irritated on a daily basis due to a feng shui solution, then you should not keep it. For example, you decide to hang a wind chime over your stove to attract prosperity. However, you have always despised wind chimes. Therefore, every time you look up and see it, you are annoyed. This situation is clearly not helping you. You can stimulate your finances in another way. In general, disliking an enhancement is worse feng shui than abandoning it altogether. The objective is to choose a feng shui remedy that appeals to you. As you have discovered, numerous enhancements are offered throughout the book. Choose the ones that speak to you and uplift your environment.

BELOW: Rejuvenate any room with colors that brighten your spirit. Good feng shui living urges you to dine gloriously, eating your favorite foods off your best china.

tip three—the importance of perspective

You have many aspects to consider when applying the energy techniques. First, decide what you need or wish to focus on. Secondly, analyze your space to formulate the best plan to achieve your goal. At times, you may feel as if there is no way to make a specific arrangement work. The shape of the room, size of the furniture, closets, windows, or the way the space is laid out may not be feasible. Don't fret. If you can make it work, fantastic! If a certain adjustment is out of the question, just move on to the next. Feng shui is meant to be restorative. Please, don't rush and don't stress. You have the rest of your life to continue manifesting your dreams. Allow your creative process to flourish and to follow its course.

RIGHT: Add flourishing plants, vivid colors, and natural light to increase energy and strengthen the bagua in every room.

tip four—stagnating energy

Check in with your feng shui enhancements every six months. Evaluate your circumstances. How are your finances? Your children? Your job? Determine if you need to make any additional adjustments or enhancements. Your life is continually changing, and your feng shui should be modified as your priorities shift. Return to the questions in chapter two and answer them again. Remember that healthy energy is moving energy. Move items around to activate fresh energy. Mix and match positive symbols in various areas of the home. Remember that you can always add a plant for extra energy. The exception is, of course, when clutter is rampant.

tip five—feng shui dining

Feng shui exists inside of you. You can expand your vision and achieve greater results by taking it beyond the home and workspace. To empower yourself, implement the philosophy and techniques in your daily comings and goings. Feng shui promotes the principles and the use of energy, positive symbols, harmony, and flow wherever you are.

Dining at restaurants takes on an entirely new meaning after you learn the principles of feng shui. In becoming aware of the effect your surroundings have on you, you can use feng shui to determine the best table to enjoy

your meal. Obviously, you don't want to become obsessed about which table you occupy. However, maximizing the energy you are receiving is beneficial regardless where you are.

Pointers for a pleasurable dining experience:
- Avoid sitting at a table in a direct line with the door, at the bottom of a staircase, or directly outside the restroom.
- Avoid sitting at a table where a protruding corner of a wall or the sharp edge of furniture is pointing at you.
- Sit with your back to a wall so that you have a view of the entire room.
- Request a table next to the window for a beautiful view, close to the fireplace, or near a plant to lift your mood.

BELOW: Create a feng shui travel kit with incense, inspirational books, silk fabric, a journal, a photo of loved ones, and your favorite music.

tip six—feng shui travel

If you are planning to stay at a hotel for business or for pleasure, you can apply feng shui to your room. You need to keep your energy at peak level whether you are at home or out of town. The amount of feng shui you implement depends on the length of your stay and the size of your suitcase. Many people assemble a feng shui travel kit to take with them wherever they go. Eventually, as you begin to live your life using more positive energy, these techniques will become second nature.

Here is a list of suggestions for vacation travel, business trips, and family gatherings. You will notice a big difference as you energize the room and personalize it with your own belongings. Create a homey environment even for a few nights.

enhancements for a hotel room
Feel free to incorporate as many or few as you like. Items to pack in your suitcase:
- Small scented candles
- Essential bath oils

- Incense and incense holder
- Favorite music
- Small picture of partner or family
- Scarf or fabric
- Inspirational books
- Personal spiritual object
- Writing journal
- Portable tape recorder or personal radio with small speakers

purchases

Once you reach your hotel, you may want to purchase these items:

- Flowering plant to add color and energy
- Salt for a salt bath
- Fresh flowers (ask the hotel for a vase)

feng shui in your hotel room

The following are some ways to apply the principles of feng shui to your hotel room:

- Ask for a room with a pleasant view, preferably far away from busy elevators, stairwells, and outside traffic or construction. One side of the hotel is always superior to the other.
- Close the bathroom door and put the toilet lid down to keep money in your pockets.
- Drape a scarf or fabric over sharp corners coming from night tables and bureaus. You can also use a towel from the bathroom.
- Burn incense to clear energy from prior guests. Open the windows to allow fresh air to circulate.
- Place personal pictures, books, candles, and special objects around the room.
- Turn on your music to relax, uplift, and enchant.
- Place a plant or flowers on a table or dresser to harmonize energy and to add color and fragrance.
- Before retiring, cover any mirrors that reflect your image in bed.
- Turn the television off and close the cabinet before going to sleep.

tip seven—considerations for a new home

Are you planning to move into a new house, apartment, or condominium? To find a home that emanates good feng shui, use the questions listed below. You might want to write them down to take with you on your search for a new home. Take notes regarding the favorable and less beneficial characteristics as you look at different possibilities. If you have found a fabulous space that is not ideal feng shui, remember that you can remedy and enhance most problem areas. Refer to the specific chapters for solutions and enhancements. Determine your priorities and move forward slowly with clear intention.

- What type of energy is coming towards the front door? Is there a T-junction? Is the home located at a dead end street? Are there sharp corners? Who are your neighbors? Does the home have potential for beautiful landscaping (See chapter seven.)?

- What do you know about the prior tenants? Did they suffer from a long illness? Did someone die? Was there a divorce? Did the people in the home experience some sort of misfortune? (See chapters one and three.)

- Does the space have any missing centers or lucky extensions? Is the house irregularly shaped? If it is missing the Wealth, Love, or Career centers, are you confident that you can fix them properly? (See chapter five.)

- Does the front door line up with a back door or window? (See chapter seven)

- Does the staircase lead to the front door or to the center of the home? (See chapter seven.)

- Where are the bathrooms located in terms of the bagua? Are they draining energy in significant centers such as Wealth, Health, Love, or Career? Is a bathroom located in the center, at or above the entrance, sharing a wall with your potential bed location, or above the stove? (See chapters five and eight.)

- Are the ceilings slanted? Do they have exposed beams? Do the rooms have protruding corners? Pay special attention to the bedrooms. (See chapters eight and nine.)

- Does the home have enough natural light? Will sunlight stream through the windows? This helps to determine if plants will grow and if you will be exposed to enough daylight on a daily basis to feel energized. (See chapters four, eight and nine.)

- Stand in the space and close your eyes. What is your first instinct? Will you be happy living here? (See chapter two.)

RIGHT: A thriving garden reveals the love and care taken by previous owners. Inheriting their good fortune increases your chances for a happy, successful future in your new home.

feng shui short cuts

These "musts" are the best gifts I can offer you. If you want to concentrate on a specific area of your life, begin with these short cuts. Below are recommendations for increased health, love, and wealth. After each one, you will find the chapter explaining each solution or enhancement. Refer to them for additional clarification and detailed instructions.

tip eight—ten musts for health

- Clear clutter everywhere, especially in your bedroom, under your bed, and in the foyer. (See chapters three, seven, and eight.)
- Make sure your bed is not under a window, sharing a wall with a toilet, or at the end of a long hallway. Move your bed out from underneath exposed beams and away from sharp corners. Purchase a new mattress if you or your companion has experienced a prolonged illness in the bed. (See chapter eight.)
- Energize any bathroom in the center of the house. Make sure a bathroom is not sharing a wall with your stove. Close all bathroom doors and lower toilet lids. (See chapters five and eight.)
- Cover all mirrors that reflect your image when you are in bed. Close the bathroom door in the master bedroom to avoid contamination while you sleep. (See chapter eight.)
- Energize the Health center of your home with a plant and with yellow items. (See chapters five and six.)
- Create a Health manifestation board to hang in the bedroom or center of the home. Make sure you can see it every day. Place notes around your house, affirming your excellent health. Display healthy photos of yourself. (See chapters five, six, and eight.)
- Add plants and light everywhere to harmonize and uplift energy. Open the windows to let fresh air in. Use full-spectrum bulbs to simulate sunlight. (See chapter four.)

ABOVE: Natural sunlight uplifts energy in the home, elevates your mood, and strengthens your overall health and vitality. Create a seating area where you can absorb its healing effects.

- Add a water element to harmonize your health if you have a fireplace in the center of your home. (See chapter six.)
- Remove excess electronic equipment from your home. Avoid keeping electronics in the bedroom. Counteract the electromagnetic rays coming from your computer by adding plants and a radiation screen to the monitor. (See chapters eight and ten.)
- Meditate, absorb tree energy, and cut the cords from negative situations and upsetting people. Practice forgiveness. Give money to an organization of your choice in the name of your excellent health. (See chapter two.)

RIGHT: Invest in rounded or curved furniture like this beautiful chair and the table behind. When possible, diffuse energy created by sharp corners by covering the corner with a silk tablecloth or perching a plant on top to soften the edges.

tip nine—ten musts for love

- Clear clutter everywhere, especially in the bedroom and Love and Relationship centers. (See chapters three, five, and eight.)

- Energize a bathroom located in the Love and Relationship center. Close the door and lower the toilet lid. (See chapters five, six, and eight.)

- Remove items from a past relationship or anything that reminds you of it. Avoid sleeping on a mattress that you shared with a former partner from a long-term relationship. Now is the time for new energy. (See chapters two, six, and eight.)

- Energize the Love and Relationship corner of the house and in your bedroom with a plant, light, and personal love anchors. (See chapters six and eight.)

- Remove all pictures and images that depict one person or one thing. Pair items together in your home such as two candles, two picture frames, two night tables, two people in a photo, or a picture of two flowers. (See chapters six and eight.)

- Hang a romantic picture across from your bed to gaze at before you fall asleep and the moment you awaken. (See chapter eight.)

- Create a romantic, sensual bedroom to usher in a new love interest. Add pink, peach, and red to the bedroom and to the Love and Relationship center. (See chapter eight.)

- Make a Love manifestation board for the bedroom or Love and Relationship corner. (See chapters six and eight.)

- Add a water element to harmonize and calm the fire energy if you have a fireplace in your Love and Relationships center. (See chapters six and eight.)

- Create loving energy around you by intentionally sending pink light to potential love interests. Write a list of qualities you want your new mate to possess. Cultivate an attitude of gratitude about the love you already have and notice it wherever you go. Expect and prepare for the right person to manifest in your life. (See chapter two.)

ABOVE: Red accents in a setting of fragrant flowers, vibrant décor and sensual artwork inspire love and passion in the home.

ABOVE RIGHT: Energize a bathroom in the Wealth & Prosperity center with a plant, water fountain, and the color red.

BELOW RIGHT: Hang a crystal and position a large stabilizer at the base of a stairwell to diminish financial loss created by energy racing towards the front door. A curved staircase moderates the flow of energy; green symbolizes money.

tip ten—ten musts for wealth

- Clear clutter in your home, office, and all Wealth centers. (See chapters three, six, and ten.)
- Energize your bathroom if it's in the Wealth center; you could be losing money. Be sure to close all bathroom doors and lower the toilet lids. (See chapters five, six, and eight.)
- Place a water fountain, plant, and light in the Wealth center of your home, living room, and office. (See chapters five, six, nine, and ten.)
- Create a Wealth manifestation board and place it in the Wealth center or someplace where you can see it daily. (See chapter five.)
- Hang a crystal if your front door opens to a staircase or to a direct view of a window or the back door. Place the crystal halfway between your front door and the staircase, window, or back door. The crystal should be at least two inches below the top of the door frame. (See chapter seven.)
- Add items in red and gold to the Wealth center and office. (See chapters five, six, and ten.)
- Align your desk in the correct power position and hang an inspiring picture across from it. Avoid sitting with your back to a window. Do not position your desk to share a wall with a toilet. (See chapters eight and ten.)
- Make sure your stove is in good working order. Double the energy of the burners by placing a mirror to reflect them. Hang a wind chime above your head as you cook. Take water off the stove after you finish cooking unless the stove is located in the center of the home. (See chapter nine.)
- Buy a new wallet and place your paycheck in a red envelope for twenty-four hours before depositing it in your bank account. (See chapter ten.)
- Donate money on a regular basis. Create good karma and prosperity consciousness simultaneously. Remember, what goes around, comes around. (See chapter two.)

tip eleven—your new wisdom

Inspire your family, friends, and coworkers with simple feng shui techniques. Give tips regarding bathrooms, sharp edges, plants, vibrant colors, and positive symbols to anyone who is receptive. You might offer to show a friend where the Health, Wealth, Career, and Relationship centers are located in their home. Be creative by giving feng shui gifts for birthdays, anniversaries, weddings, and holidays. You might want to give a plant in a colorful pot, scented candles, a tabletop water fountain, a silk or live flower arrangement, a positive symbol for wealth, an inspiring piece of art, or a book on feng shui.

the extraordinary gift of energy

My intention in writing this book was to inspire, motivate, and empower you to transform your life. I encourage you to use the energy techniques wisely and properly. Continue to give as you receive. The gifts of love, service, and resources bestowed upon others will come back to you multiplied many times.

I hope that feng shui propels you to live passionately, purposefully, and harmoniously in your surroundings. Remember to breathe, use your intuition, go with the flow, and have fun!

Open your heart and mind to the unseen and the unexpected. The benefits of feng shui are immeasurable. I send you an abundance of love, gratitude, and fortunate energy. Thank you for joining me on this journey. I am quite sure your successful energy blueprint is in the works.

RIGHT: Flowing into the ocean and uniting with the sky, an infinity pool symbolizes vast opportunity. With your newly acquired feng shui knowledge and power, you're ready to grasp that opportunity and design your destiny.

index

interior design credits

Anderson Papachristidis Raeymakers
Interiors, (212) 588-1777: pp.18, 265

Antonia Hutt and Associates, Inc. (323)
932-0511: pp. 188, 239, 247

D'Aquino Monaco, Inc., (212) 929-9787:
pp. 105 (bottom), 106, 162

Diamond and Barratta, (212) 966-8892:
pp. 103, 179, 183, 199, 213, 219, 224, 269

KWID, (323) 951-7454: pp. 234, 266; 268

Linda Marder, (323) 656-8844: pp. 105
(top), 217

Luis Ortega Design Studio, (310) 358-
0211: pp. 95, 242, 250

McAlpine Tankersley Architecture, (334)
262-8315 /McAlpine Booth and Ferrier
Interiors, (615) 259-1222: p. 61

Miles Redd LLC, (212) 995-1922: p. 218

Nancy Braithwaite Interiors, (404) 355-
1740: pp. 34, 195, 223

Oetgen Design, (404) 352-1112: p. 69

Plantation, (323) 932-0511: pp. 193, 241

Sheldon Mindell Associates, (212) 243-
3939: pp. 21, 32, 39, 62, 77, 118, 252

Steven Shubel Design, Inc., (415) 925-
9332: table of contents; pp.25, 65, 104,
203, 216, 264

Tsao McKown, (212) 337-3800: cover; pp.
98, 185

Victoria Montana for Nancy Corzine, (310)
652-4500: p. 257

Vincente Wolf Associates, Inc., (212) 465-
0590: p. 91